[S.S. 306.]  Ia/38390.

NOTES

ON

GERMAN FUZES

AND

TYPICAL FRENCH AND BELGIAN FUZES.

(SECOND EDITION.)

General Staff (Intelligence),
    General Headquarters,
        1st January, 1918.

The Naval & Military Press Ltd

Published by the
The Naval & Military Press
in association with the Royal Armouries

Unit 10 Ridgewood Industrial Park,
Uckfield, East Sussex, TN22 5QE
Tel: +44 (0) 1825 749494
Fax: +44 (0) 1825 765701

MILITARY HISTORY AT YOUR FINGERTIPS
www.naval-military-press.com

ONLINE GENEALOGY RESEARCH
www.military-genealogy.com

ONLINE MILITARY CARTOGRAPHY
www.militarymaproom.com

ROYAL ARMOURIES

The Library & Archives Department at the Royal Armouries Museum, Leeds, specialises in the history and development of armour and weapons from earliest times to the present day. Material relating to the development of artillery and modern fortifications is held at the Royal Armouries Museum, Fort Nelson.

For further information contact:
Royal Armouries Museum, Library, Armouries Drive,
Leeds, West Yorkshire LS10 1LT
Royal Armouries, Library, Fort Nelson, Down End Road, Fareham PO17 6AN

Or visit the Museum's website at
www.armouries.org.uk

In reprinting in facsimile from the original, any imperfections are inevitably reproduced and the quality may fall short of modern type and cartographic standards.

CONTENTS.

	PAGE.
List of German artillery fuzes	3
Table showing fuzes used with various guns, howitzers and "Minenwerfer"	6
Marks on German fuzes	14
Manufacturers' marks	14
Distinguishing marks	15
Abbreviations used in connection with German ordnance and ammunition	16
Material of German fuzes	19
Percussion fuzes	20
Time and percussion fuzes	90
Fuzes for universal shell	132
Obsolete artillery fuzes	136
Naval fuzes—	
(a) Percussion fuzes	142
(b) Time and percussion fuzes	158
"Minenwerfer" fuzes—	
(a) Percussion fuzes	170
(b) Time and percussion fuzes	180
Typical French fuzes	196
Typical Belgian fuzes	204
Appendix I.—Conversion table: Inches to millimetres	217
Appendix II.—Conversion table: Yards to metres	218
Appendix III.—Conversion table: Metres to yards	219

LIST OF GERMAN ARTILLERY FUZES NOW IN USE IN LAND WARFARE.

Percussion Fuzes.—

	PAGE
3·7 cm. Gr. Z.	20
5 cm. Gr. Z.	22
K.Z. 14	24
K.Z. 14 n.A.	24
L.K.Z. 16 o.V.	26
L.K.Z. 16 m.V.	26
K.Z. 16 m.V.	28
E.K.Z. 16	30
E.K.Z. 16 C.	32
E.K.Z. 17	34
Anti-tank fuze	36
H.Z. 14	44
H.Z. 14 Fliehb. (*or* Fb.)	46
H.Z. 14 Vorst.	46
H.Z. 14 Vorst. Fliehb. (*or* Fb.)	46
H.Z. 16	48
E.H.Z. 16	50
E.H.Z. 16 C.	52
E.H.Z. 17	54
K.Z. 16 f. 10 cm. K.	56
Gr. Z. 82	64
Gr. Z. 92	66
Gr. Z. 04	68
Gr. Z. 14	70
Gr. Z. 14 n.A.	72
Gr. Z. 17	74
lg. Bd. Z. 10	82
Brd. Gesch. lg. Bd. Z. 10	82
kz. Bd. Z. 10	84
kz. Bd. Z. 10 Kst. K.	84

Time and Percussion Fuzes.—

	PAGE
Dopp. Z. 96 n/A.	90
K.Z. 11 Gr.	92
K.Z. 11 Gr. l.B.	92
L.K.Z. 11 Gr.	94
H.Z. 05 Gr.	102
H.Z. 05 Gr. l.B.	102

Time and Percussion Fuzes—*continued.*

H.Z. 05 Schr.	... 104
Lg. Zdr. S/22	... 106
Dopp. Z. 92	... 114
{ Dopp. Z. 92 f. 10 cm. K.	116
{ Dopp. Z. 92 K. 15	... 116
Dopp. Z. 92 lg. Brlg.	... 118
{ Dopp. Z. 92 lg. Brlg. n. F.	120
{ Dopp. Z. 92 n. F.	... 120
Dopp. Z. 15	... 122
Dopp. Z. 16	... 124

Fuzes for Universal Shell.—

K.Z. 11	... 132
K.Z. 11 l.B.	... 132
H.Z. 05	... 134
H.Z. 05 l.B.	... 134

OBSOLETE GERMAN ARTILLERY FUZES.

(a) Percussion Fuzes.—

Gr. Z. 84	... 136
Gr. Z. 96	... 136
Gr. Z. 96/04	... 136
Kz. Gr. Z. 14	... 138
G. Gr. Z. 14	... 138
15 cm. Gr. C/14	... 138
Bd. Z. 06	... 138

(b) Time and Percussion Fuzes.—

Dopp. Z. 86	... 139
Dopp. Z. 88	... 139
Dopp. Z. 91	... 139
Dopp. Z. 92 f. FH.	... 139
Dopp. Z. 96	... 139
Dopp. Z. 98	... 140
Dopp. Z. 08	... 140

(c) Fuzes for Universal Shell.—

K.Z. 11	... 140
H.Z. 05	... 140

NAVAL FUZES.

	PAGE.
(a) **Percussion Fuzes.—**	
Z. f. 3·7 cm. Spgr.	142
Granat-Zünder C/98	144
Percussion fuze (10·5 cm. and 15 cm. shell)	146
Percussion fuze (17 cm. shell)	148
{ Spgr. m. K.	150
{ m. V. u. K.	150
(b) **Time and Percussion Fuzes.—**	
Dopp. Z. S/26	158
Dopp. Z. S/43	160
Dopp. Z. S/56	162

"MINENWERFER" FUZES.

	PAGE.
(a) **Percussion Fuzes.—**	
Az. 16 f.l.W.M.	170
Percussion fuze (designation unknown)	172
(b) **Time and Percussion Fuzes.—**	
l. W.M. Zdr.	180
l. W.M. Zdr. 2	180
{ Z.m.W.M.	182
{ Z.s.u.m.W.M.	182
Z.s.W.M.	184
Canister bomb fuze	186
Z.gl.W.M.	188

TABLE SHOWING FUZES USED WITH VARIOUS GUNS, HOWITZERS AND "MINENWERFER."

A.—ARMY AND COAST DEFENCE GUNS.

3·7 cm. Revolver Gun (*3·7 cm. Rev. K.*).
  (Calibre = 3·7 cm. = 1·46 inches.)
  3·7 cm. Gr. Z.

5 cm. Gun on Shielded Mounting (*5 cm. K.i.P.L.*).
  (Calibre = 5·3 cm. = 2·09 inches.)
  5 cm. Gr. Z.

7·62 cm. Infantry Gun (*Converted Russian Field Gun*).
  (Calibre = 7·62 cm. = 3·0 inches.)
  K.Z. 14.
  L.K.Z. 16 m.V.

7·62 cm. Anti-Aircraft Gun (*7·62 cm. Flak.*).
  (Calibre = 7·62 cm. = 3·0 inches.)
  K.Z. 11 Gr. o.Az.

7·7 cm. Gun on Casemate Mounting (*7·7cm. K.i.Kas.L.*).
  (Calibre = 7·7 cm. = 3·03 inches.)
   K.Z. 14 (obsolescent).
   Dopp. Z 96 (obsolete).
   Dopp. Z. 96 n/A.
   K.Z. 11 (obsolete).

(7·7 cm.) **Field Gun (96 n/A.) (*F.K. 96 n/A.*).*
(7·7 cm.) **Field Gun '16 (*F.K. 16*).*
  (Calibre = 7·7 cm. = 3·03 inches.)
   K.Z. 14 (obsolete).
   K.Z. 14 m.V. (obsolete).
   K.Z. 14 n.A.
   K.Z. 16 m.V. (obsolete).
   L.K.Z. 16 o.V. (obsolete).
   L.K.Z. 16 m.V.
   E.K.Z. 16.
   E.K.Z. 16 C.
   E.K.Z. 17.
   Anti-tank fuze.
   Dopp. Z. 96 (obsolete).
   Dopp. Z. 96 n/A.
   K.Z. 11 (obsolete).
   K.Z. 11 I.B. (obsolete).
   K.Z. 11 Gr., K.Z. 11 Gr. nur Bz.
   K.Z. 11 Gr. l.B.
   L.K.Z. 11 Gr.

* Guns in common use.

*9 cm. Field Gun ('73/'88) (*9 cm. K.*).

(Calibre = 8·8 cm. = 3·46 inches.)
Gr. Z. 82 (obsolete).
Gr. Z. 14 (obsolescent).
Kz. Gr. Z. 14 (obsolete).
H.Z. 14 Vorst.
Dopp. Z. 86 (obsolete).
Dopp. Z. 91 (obsolete).
{ Dopp. Z. 92 f. 10 cm. K.
{ Dopp. Z. 92 K. 15.
Dopp. Z. 92 lg. Brlg.
{ Dopp. Z. 92 lg. Brlg. n.F.
{ Dopp. Z. 92 n.F.

9 cm. Anti-Aircraft Gun (*9 cm. B.A.K.*).

(Calibre = 8·8 cm. = 3·46 inches.)
Dopp. Z. 92 lg. Brlg. o. Az.

*(10·5 cm.) Light Field Howitzer '98/'09 (*l.F.H. 98/09*).
*(10·5 cm.) Light Field Howitzer '16 (*l.F.H. 16*).
*(10·5 cm.) Light Field Howitzer, Krupp (*l.F.H. Krupp*).

(Calibre = 10·5 cm. = 4·13 inches.)
{ H.Z. 14 (obsolete).
{ H.Z. 14 Fliehb. (*or* Fb.).
H.Z. 16.
E.H.Z. 16.
E.H.Z. 16 C.
E.H.Z. 17.
Dopp. Z. 92 für FH. (obsolete).
Dopp. Z. 98 (obsolete).
H.Z. 05 (obsolete).
H.Z. 05 l.B. (obsolete).
H.Z. 05 Gr.
H.Z. 05 Gr. l.B.
H.Z. 05 Schr.
Lg. Zdr. S/22.

10 cm. Gun '97 (*10 cm. K. 97*), **10 cm. Gun** (*10 cm. K.*), ***10 cm. Gun '04** (*10 cm. K. 04*), and ***10 cm. Gun '14** (*10 cm. K. 14*).

(Calibre = 10·5 cm. = 4·13 inches.)
Gr. Z. 04.
{ H.Z. 14 Vorst. (obsolete).
{ H.Z. 14 Vorst. Fliehb. (*or* Fb.).
K.Z. 16 f. 10 cm. K.
{ Dopp. Z. 92 f. 10 cm. K.
{ Dopp. Z. 92 K. 15.
Dopp. Z. 92 lg. Brlg.
{ Dopp. Z. 92 lg. Brlg. n.F.
{ Dopp. Z. 92 n.F.

* Guns in common use.

10 cm. Gun with Overhead Shield (*10 cm. K.i.S.L.*), **10 cm. Gun in Turret** (*10 cm. T.K.*), **10 cm. Reinforced Gun in Turret** (*10 cm. T.K. Verst.*), **10 cm. Short Gun in Turret** (*kz. 10 cm. T.K.*).

(Calibre = 10·5 cm. = 4·13 inches.).
Same fuzes as for preceding 10 cm. guns, omitting the last three fuzes.

10 cm. Coast Defence Gun (*10 cm. Kst. K.*).

(Calibre = 10·5 cm. = 4·13 inches.)
kz. Bd. Z. 10 Kst. K.

10 cm. Coast Defence Gun on Wheeled Carriage (*10 cm. Kst. K.i.R.L.*).

(Calibre = 10·5 cm. = 4·13 inches.)
kz. Bd. Z. 10 Kst. K.
Gr. Z. 04.

12 cm. Heavy Gun (*s. 12 cm. K.*).

(Calibre = 12·03 cm. = 4·73 inches.)
*H.Z. 14 Vorst.
Gr. Z. 14.
Gr. Z. 14 n.A.
Dopp. Z. 88 (obsolete).
Dopp. Z. 92.

*13 cm. Gun (*13 cm. K.*).

(Calibre = 13·5 cm. = 5·31 inches.)
lg. Bd. Z. 10.
Brd. Gesch. lg. Bd. Z. 10.
Gr. Z. 04.
{ Dopp. Z. 92 f. 10 cm. K.
{ Dopp. Z. 92 K. 15.
Dopp. Z. 92 lg. Brlg.

15 cm. Experimental Gun on Wheeled Carriage (*15 cm. Vers. K.i.R.L.*).

(Calibre = 14·97 cm. = 5·89 inches.)
Gr. Z. 04.
{ Dopp. Z. 92 f. 10 cm. K.
{ Dopp. Z. 92 K. 15.
Dopp. Z. 92 lg. Brlg.
Dopp. Z. 16.

* Guns in common use.

15 cm. Gun with Overhead Shield (*15 cm. K.i.S.L.*).

(Calibre = 14·97 cm. = 5·89 inches.)
  Gr. Z. 04.
  lg. Bd. Z. 10.
  { Dopp. Z. 92 f. 10 cm. K.
  { Dopp. Z. 92 K. 15.
  Dopp. Z. 92 lg. Brlg.
  Dopp. Z. 08 (obsolete).
  Dopp. Z. 16 (?).

15 cm. Long Gun (*lg. 15 cm. K.*).

(Calibre = 14·97 cm. = 5·89 inches.)
  Gr. Z. 96/04 (obsolete).
  Gr. Z. 04.
  Gr. Z. 14 (obsolescent).
  Gr. Z. 14 n.A.
  Dopp. Z. 92.

15 cm. Gun with Chase Rings (*15 cm. R.K.*) and **Long 15 cm. Gun with Chase Rings** (*lg. 15 cm. R.K.*).

(Calibre = 14·97 cm. = 5·89 inches.)
  Gr. Z. 96/04 (obsolete).
  Gr. Z. 04.
  Gr. Z. 14 (obsolescent).
  Gr. Z. 14 n.A.
  Dopp. Z. 92.

15 cm. Gun '07 on Coast Defence Mounting (*15 cm. K.i.Kst. L. 07*).

(Calibre = 14·97 cm. = 5·89 inches.)
  lg. Bd. Z. 10.
  { Dopp. Z. 92 f. 10 cm. K.
  { Dopp. Z. 92 K. 15.

(15 cm.) Heavy Field Howitzer (*s. F.H.*), *****(15 cm.) Heavy Field Howitzer '02** (*s. F.H. 02.*), *****(15 cm.) Heavy Field Howitzer '13** (*s.F.H.13*), *****(15 cm.) Long Heavy Field Howitzer '13** (*lg. s. F.H. 13*).

(Calibre = 14·97 cm. = 5·89 inches.)
  Gr. Z. 82.
  Gr. Zdg. 88 (obsolete).
  Gr. Z. 92.
  Gr. Z. 96/04 (obsolete).
  Gr. Z. 04.
  Gr. Z. 14 (obsolescent).
  Gr. Z. 14 n. A.
  Gr. Z. 17.
  Dopp. Z. 92.
  Dopp. Z. 92 lg. Brlg.
  { Dopp. Z. 15.
  { Dopp. Z. 15 umg.

* Guns in common use.

(15 cm.) Coast Defence Heavy Field Howitzer (*s. F.H.Kst.*).
  (Calibre = 14·97 cm. = 5·89 inches.)
    Gr. Z. 82 (Kp.).

15 cm. Howitzer in Turret (*15 cm. T.H.*).
  (Calibre = 14·97 cm. = 5·89 inches.)
    Dopp. Z. 92.

21 cm. Gun with Chase Rings (*21 cm. R.K.*).
  (Calibre = 20·93 cm. = 8·24 inches.)
    lg. Bd. Z. 10.
    Dopp. Z. 92.

21 cm. Howitzer in Turret (*21 cm. T.H.*).
  (Calibre = 20·93 cm. = 8·24 inches.)
    Gr. Z. 82 (Kp.).
    Dopp. Z. 92.

21 cm. Mortar and *" Mortar "† (*21 cm. Mrs. and Mrs.*).
  (Calibre = 21·1 cm. = 8·3 inches.)
    Bd. Z. 06 (obsolete).
    lg. Bd. Z. 10.
    kz. Bd. Z. 10.
    Gr. Z. 92.
    Gr. Z. 96/04 (obsolete).
    Gr. Z. 04.
    Gr. Z. 04/14.

21 cm. Bronze Coast Defence Mortar (*21 cm. Br. Kst. Mrs.*).
  (Calibre = 20·93 cm. = 8·24 inches.)
    lg. Bd. Z. 10.

(28 cm.) Coast Defence Howitzer on Coast Defence Howitzer Carriage (*Kst. H.i.Kst. H.L.*).
  (Calibre = 28·0 cm.(?) = 11·02 inches.)
    lg. Bd. Z. 10.
    kz. Bd. Z. 10.

*42 cm. Howitzer (   ).
  (Calibre = 42·0 cm.(?) = 16·5 inches).
    kz. Bd. Z. 10.

---

* Guns in common use.
† 21 cm. mortar is the older pattern; the latest pattern, introduced in 1910, is called " Mortar " (" *Mörser*") without specifying the calibre.

B.—NAVAL GUNS.

3·7 cm. Trench Gun. (*3·7 cm. Schützengraben K.*)
  (Calibre = 3·7 cm. = 1·46 inches.)
    Z.f. 3·7 cm. Spgr.

6 cm. B.L. Boat Gun L/21.
6 cm. Q.F. Boat Gun L/21.
  (Calibre = 6 cm. = 2·36 inches.)
  Time and percussion fuze.

8·8 cm. Q.F. Guns L/30, L/35 and L/45 (*8·8 cm. S.K. L/30, L/35, L/45*).
  (Calibre = 8·8 cm. = 3·46 inches.)
  Granatzünder C/89.
  Granatzünder m.V. (Internal fuze.)
  Dopp. Z. S/26.

10·5 cm. Q.F. Gun L/35 (*10·5 cm. S.K. L/35, or s. 10 cm. K.*).
  (Calibre = 10·5 cm. = 4·13 inches.)
  Percussion fuze (designation unknown).
  Dopp. Z. S/43.

15 cm. Gun L/30 (*15 cm.K.L/30*).
  (Calibre = 14·97 cm. = 5·89 inches.)
  Gr. Z. 04.
  Gr. Z. 14 (obsolescent).
  Dopp. Z. S/43.

*15 cm. Q.F. Gun L/40 (*15 cm. S.K. L/40, or s. 15 cm. K.*).
  (Calibre = 14·97 cm. = 5·89 inches.)
  Percussion fuze (designation unknown).
  Dopp. Z. S/43.
  Dopp. Z. S/56 (?).

17 cm. Q.F. Gun L/40 (*17 cm. S.K.L/40*).
  (Calibre = 17·2 cm. (?) = 6·77 inches.)
  Percussion fuze (designation unknown).

21 cm. Q.F. Gun L/45 (*21 cm. S.K. L/45*).
  (Calibre = 20·93 cm. (?) = 8·24 inches.)
  Spgr. m.K.

* Guns in common use.

24 cm. Q.F. Gun on Fixed Mounting (*24 cm. Bettungskanone*).

*24 cm. Q.F. Gun L/40 on Railway Mounting (*24 cm. S.K. L/40, auf Eisenbahnwagen*).

(Calibre = 23·6 cm.(?) = 9·29 inches.)
Spgr. m.K.
Dopp. Z. 16.

28 cm. Q.F. Guns L/40, L/45, and L/50 (*28 cm. S.K. L/40, L/45, L/50*).

(Calibre = 28·0 cm.(?) = 11·02 inches.)

30·5 cm. Q.F. Guns L/45 and L/50 (*30·5 cm. S.K. L/45, L/50*).

(Calibre = 30·5 cm.(?) = 12 inches.)

35·6 cm. Gun.

(Calibre = 35·6 cm. = 14 inches.)
Spgr. m.K.

*38 cm. Gun L/45.

(Calibre = 38·1 cm.(?) = 15 inches.)
$\begin{cases} \text{Spgr. m.K.} \\ \text{m.V.u.K.} \end{cases}$

Guns in common use.

C. "MINENWERFER."

*(7·6† cm.) Light "Minenwerfer" (*l.M.W.a.A.*).
(7·6 cm.) New Light "Minenwerfer" (*l.M.W.n.A.*).
  (Calibre = 7·6 cm. = 2·99 inches.)
  Az. 16. f.l.W.M.

  l.W.M. Zdr.
  l.W.M. Zdr. 2.

*(17 cm.) Medium "Minenwerfer" (*m.M.W.*).
  (Calibre = 17 cm. = 6·69 inches.)

  Z.m.W.M.
  Z.s.u.m.W.M.

(17 cm.) Medium "Minenwerfer" '16 (*m.M.W. 16*).

*(25 cm.) Heavy "Minenwerfer" (*s.M.W.*).
  (Calibre = 25 cm. = 9·84 inches.)

  Z.s.W.M.
  Z.s.u.m.W.M.

(25 cm.) Heavy "Minenwerfer" '16 (*s.M.W. 16*).

(24 cm.) Heavy "Flügelminenwerfer."
  Percussion fuze (delay action).
  Percussion fuze (non-delay action).

(18 cm.) Smooth-bore "Minenwerfer."
  Z. gl. W.M.
  Z.s.u.m.W.M.

(25 cm.) Heavy "Ladungswerfer" Ehrhardt.
  Canister bomb fuze.

* *Minenwerfer* in common use.
† This is the calibre of the trench mortar: the calibre of the shell is 7·55 cm

MARKS ON GERMAN FUZES.

Practically all German fuzes are clearly marked with the designation of the fuze (which includes the year of introduction), followed by the distinguishing letter or mark of the establishment where it was manufactured and the year of manufacture. For example, the fuze shown on page 35 is marked—

E.K.Z. 17.
A.E.G. 17.

This stands for *Empfindlicher Kanonen-Zünder, 1917. Allgemeine Electricitäts-Gesellschaft*, meaning "instantaneous gun fuze of the 1917 pattern, manufactured by the General Electrical Co. in 1917."

In addition to these marks, most fuzes have a factory series number, *e.g.*, "141e" on the above-mentioned fuze.

Manufacturers' Marks.—

Fuzes are manufactured at arsenals, and also by a very large number of private firms.

Manufacturers' marks play no part in the identification of shells and guns, but a few of the better-known trade marks are given below for information.

Dn.	=	Danzig.
Dr.	=	Dresden.
J.	=	Ingoldstadt.
L.	=	Lubenstadt.
Sb.	=	Strassburg.
Sg.	=	Siegburg.
Sp.	=	Spandau.

} Arsenals.

A.E.G.	=	Allgemeine Electricitäts-Gesellschaft.
B.	=	Bergmann-Dynamos, Berlin.
D.W.M.	=	Deutsche Waffen und Munitions-Fabrik.
Kr.	=	Krupp.
₤	=	Ludwig Loewe & Co., Berlin.
M.A.N. or MAXVA	=	Maschinen Fabrik Augsburg-Nürnberg Aktiengesellschaft.
N.S.U.	=	Neckarsulmer Gesellschaft.
R.F.	=	Remscheid Fabrik.
R.M.F. or ⊘	=	Rheinische Metallwaren und Maschinen Fabrik.
R. Stock & Co. Simson		} German firms.
S.N.	=	Steffens Nölle, Essen.
⌘	=	Siemens-Martin.
⌬	=	Siemens-Schuckert.

} Private firms.

Distinguishing marks.—

Mark.	Fuze.	Signification.
Green cap	Gr. Z. 04	Body of fuze made of zinc and iron (*Eisenarmierung*).
Green cap	Dopp. Z. 92 lg. Brlg.	Time rings graduated up to 42 (?) seconds.
Green cap	H.Z. 14	"Green Cross" gas shell.
All green·	E.K.Z. 17... ... E.H.Z. 17... ...	} "Yellow Cross" gas shell.
Green and yellow ...	Gr. Z. 14 n.A. ...	"Green Cross" gas shell.
Yellow cap	K.Z. 11 Gr. ..	Fuze for A.A. shell; without percussion system.
Cap painted red and * or o after the designation	H.Z. 14 Fb. ... H.Z. 14 Vorst. ... K.Z. 14 ... ... Gr. Z. 14 ... ... Gr. Z. 14 n.A. ...	Detonator of superior quality.
Red cap	Dopp. Z. 92 ...	Clamping device for time ring.
"Fb." *or* "Fliehb." after the designation	H.Z. 14 Vorst. ... H.Z. 14	} *Fliehbolzen* = centrifugal bolt to secure percussion pellet.
"o.Az." after the designation	Dopp. Z. 92 lg. Brlg. o.Az.	*Ohne Aufschlagzündung*=no percussion arrangement (only for use against aircraft).
"umg" after the designation	Dopp. Z. 15 ...	Variation of.
"K. 15" after the designation	Dopp. Z. 92 K. 15	Employment same as for *Dopp. Z. 92 f. 10 cm. K.*
* above the designations "lg. Bd. Z. 10" and "kz. Bd. Z. 10"	Bd. Z. 10 ...	Detonator in percussion pellet specially protected.
"n. A." or "n/A." after the designation	K.Z. 14 n.A. .. Gr. Z. 14 n.A. ...	} Of new design.
"l.B." after the designation	K.Z. 11 l.B. ... H.Z. 05 l.B. ... H.Z. 05 Gr. l.B. ...	} Long-burning fuze.
"Gr." as part of the designation	K.Z. 11 Gr. ... H.Z. 05 Gr. ...	} Simplified type of "universal shell" fuze for H.E. shell.
✛ on cap of fuze ...	E.K.Z. 17... ... E.H.Z. 17... ...	Gas shell.
"K." on time ring ...	Dopp. Z. 96 n/A....	*Kartätsche*=Setting mark for case shot effect.
G. S.	K.Z. 11	Setting marks: G.=*Granate* or H.E. effect. S.=*Schrapnel* or shrapnel effect.
✝	All time and percussion fuzes.	Cross = setting mark for percussion effect.
♔ M		Distinguishing mark stamped on all shells and fuzes of naval origin.

ABBREVIATIONS USED IN CONNECTION WITH GERMAN ORDNANCE AND AMMUNITION.

Abbreviation.	Signification.	English equivalent.
a/A.	alter Art	Of old pattern.
Az.	Aufschlag-Zünder	Percussion fuze.
Bl.	Blind	Blind.
Bz.	Brenn-Zünder	Time fuze.
Bd. G. / Brd. Gesch.	} Brand-Geschoss	} Incendiary shell.
Brand-Gr.	Brand-Granate	
Br. Mrs.	Bronze-Mörser	Bronze mortar.
Bd. Z.	Boden-Zünder	Base fuze.
C/92	Construction/92	1892 pattern.
D.Z. or Dz. / Dopp. Z.	} Doppel-Zünder	Time and percussion fuze.
Ec.	Eisen-Centrierung	With rear driving band only.
f. 10 cm. K.	für 10 cm. Kanone	For 10 centimetre gun.
E.H.Z.	Empfindlicher Haubitz-Zünder	Sensitive, *i.e.*, instantaneous howitzer fuze.
E.K.Z.	Empfindlicher Kanonen-Zünder	Sensitive, *i.e.*, instantaneous gun fuze.
Fb. / Fliehb.	} Fliehbolzen	Centrifugal bolt.
Fest.	Festung	Fortress.
F. Gr.	Feld-Granate	Field gun H.E. shell.
FH.	Feld-Haubitze	Field howitzer.
F. K.	Feld-Kanone	Field gun.
F.Patr.	Feld-Patrone	Field gun cartridge (fixed ammunition).
Fp.02	Füllpulver 02	1902 pattern explosive (T.N.T.).
Fp. $\frac{60}{40}$	Füllpulver $\frac{60}{40}$	Amatol $\frac{40}{60}$ *i.e.*, 40 per cent. ammonium nitrate and 60 per cent. T.N.T.
G.	Granate	H.E. shell.
Gel.	Geladen	Loaded.
Gesch.	{ Geschütz / Geschoss	Gun. / Projectile.
Gf.	{ Geschütz-Fabrik / Geschoss-Fabrik	Gun factory. / Shell factory.
G.g.	Granate-Geschoss	} H.E. shell.
Gr.	Granate	
Grf.88	Granatfüllung 88	1888 pattern explosive (picric acid).
Gr. Z.	Granat-Zünder	Fuze for H.E. shell.
H. Gr.	Haubitz-Granate	Howitzer shell.
H. Schr.	Haubitz-Schrapnel	Howitzer shrapnel.
H.Z.	Haubitz-Zünder	Howitzer fuze.
i.Kas.L.	in Kasemattenlafette	On casemate mounting.
i.Kst.L.	in Küstenlafette	On coast defence mounting.
i.P.L.	in Panzerlafette	On shielded mounting.
i.R.L.	in Rad-Lafette	On wheeled carriage.
i. S.L.	in Schirmlafette	On carriage with overhead shield.
Iz.	Innen-Zünder	Internal fuze (naval).
K.	Kanone	Gun.

Abbreviation.	Signification.	English equivalent.
K.	Kürzer	Shorter.
K. Kt.	} Kartätsche	Case shot.
Kart.	Kartusche	Cartridge.
K. Gr.	Kanonen-Granate	Gun shell.
K.i.H.	Kanone in Haubitzlafette	Gun on howitzer mounting.
Kp.	Kappe	Cap (to cover fuze).
Kst.	Küste	Coast (defence).
Kst. H.	Küsten-Haubitze	Coast defence howitzer.
Kst. K.	Küsten-Kanone	Coast defence gun.
Kst. Mrs.	Küsten-Mörser	Coast defence mortar.
K.Z.	Kanonen-Zünder	Gun fuze.
Kz.	Kopf-Zünder	Nose fuze (naval).
kz. Bd. Z.	kurzer Boden-Zünder	Short base fuze.
lg. Bd. Z.	langer Boden-Zünder	Long base fuze.
L. or l.	Leicht (e-er)	Light.
L.	Lang or Länger	Long or Longer.
l. B. lg. Brlg.	} lange Brennlänge	Long-burning (fuze)
Lggr.	Langgranate	Long shell.
Lg.Zdr.	Leuchtgeschoss-Zünder	Fuze for star shell.
L.K.Z.	Langer Kanonen-Zünder	Long fuze for gun.
l. N. M.	leichte Nachrichten-Mine	Light "Minenwerfer" message shell.
l. Spr. M.	leichte Spreng-Mine	Light "Minenwerfer" H.E. shell.
l. W. M. Zdr.	leichter Wurf-Mine-Zünder	Fuze for light "Minenwerfer" shell.
L/3.1, etc.	Used in the nomenclature of projectiles to indicate that the length is 3·1, etc., calibres.	
L/40, etc.	Used in the nomenclature of guns to indicate that the length is 40, etc., calibres.	
Mdlchb.	Mundlochbüchse	Old pattern type of fuze.
Mdlchf.	Mundlochfutter	Gaine.
m.Ozdg.	mit Oberzündung	With overhead ignition.
m.P.	mit Panzerkopf	With armour-piercing head.
Mrs.	Mörser	Mortar.
Mtl. K.	Mantel-Kanone	Jacketed gun.
M.V. or m.V.	Mit Verzögerung	With delay action.
m.v.F.	mit vorderem Führungsring	With forward driving band.
m.V.u.K.	mit Verzögerung und Klappensicherung	With delay action and centrifugal safety device.
M.W.	Minenwerfer	"Minenwerfer" (trench mortar).
n/A. or n.A.	neuer Art	Of new pattern.
n.F.	neuer Form	Of new shape.
o.Az.	ohne Aufschlagzündung	Without percussion system.
O.V. or o.V.	Ohne Verzögerung	Without delay action (non-delay action).
P.	Pulver	Powder (usually black powder).
Patr.	Patrone	Cartridge (fixed ammunition).

Abbreviation.	Signification.	English equivalent.
Rev. K. ...	Revolver-Kanone	Revolver gun.
R.K.	Ring-Kanone	Gun with chase rings.
S.	Schwer (e-er)...	Heavy.
S/43	43 Sekunden	43 seconds.
S.	} Schrapnel	Shrapnel.
Sch.		
Schr.		
Sek.	Sekunden	Seconds.
S.K.	Schnellade-Kanone	Q.F. gun.
Spgr.	} Spreng-Granate	H.E. shell.
Sprgr.		
Spgr. m.K. ...	Sprenggranatenzünder mit Klappensicherung	Fuze with centrifugal safety device for H.E. shell
T.H.	Turm-Haubitze	Howitzer in turret.
T.K.	Turm-Kanone...	Gun in turret.
U.	Unterrichts-	Instructional.
Üb.	Übungs-	Practice.
Übgr.	Übungsgranate	Practice shell.
Üb.Ldg.... ...	Übungs-Ladung	Practice charge.
Umg.	Umgeändert or umgearbeitet	Converted.
92 umg.	1892 umgeändert	} 1892 pattern converted.
92 transf. ...	1892 transformiert (?) ...	
V.	Verzögerung	Delay.
Vers.	Versuchs-	Experimental.
Verst.	Verstärkt	Strengthened.
V.K.	Verkürzte Kammerhülse ...	Shortened central tube (of shrapnel).
Vrst.	} Vorstecker	Safety pin (on fuze).
Vst.		
Vorst.		
W.M.	Wurf-Mine	Trench mortar projectile.
Z.	} Zünder	Fuze.
Zdr.		
Zdg.	Zündung	Fuze.
Zdldg.	} Zündladung	Exploder.
Zdlg.		
Z.gl.W.M. ...	Zünder glatter Wurf-Mine ...	Fuze for smooth - bore "Minenwerfer" shell.
Z.m.W.M. ...	Zünder mittlerer Wurf-Mine	Fuze for medium "Minenwerfer" shell
Z.s.W.M. ...	Zünder schwerer Wurf-Mine	Fuze for heavy "Minenwerfer" shell.
Z.s.u.m.W.M. ...	Zünder schwerer und mittlerer Wurf-Mine	Fuze for heavy and medium "Minenwerfer" shell.

MATERIAL OF GERMAN FUZES.

The materials used in several German fuzes have been analysed and the following are some typical results of the analysis :—

Fuze bodies of brass.

Fuze	H.Z. 14.	Gr. Z. 92.	l.W.M. Zdr. 2.	Dopp. Z. 15.
Manufacture	AEG 1915.	1916.	1916.	O.P. 1917.
Copper	58·97	57·40	60·0	57·3
Zinc	38·58	40·32	37·5	41·3
Lead	2·16	1·60	2·0	...
Tin	0·17	0·25	0·2	0·2
Iron	0·12	0·40	0·2	0·2
Aluminium	...	...	0·1	...

Aluminium fuzes.

Fuze	K.Z. 14.	K Z. 14.	K.Z. 14.	H.Z. 05.	K.Z. 11 Gr.	L. K.Z. 11 Gr.
Manufacture	AEG 1914.	AEG 1915.	R.Stock &Co. 1915.	Sb. 1914.	1916.	Sb. 1917.
				Time rings.	Time rings.	Time rings.
Lead	...	...	...	...	0·50	...
Copper	2·22	1·74	2·20	2·20	2·40	2·54
Tin	5·22	6·82	4·14	3·42	4·60	...
Zinc	...	...	...	...	1·00	1·42
Iron	0·30	0·48	0·56	0·52	0·67	1·78
Silicon	0·30	0·36	0·69	0·19	0·20	0·76
Aluminium	91·96	90·60	92·41	93·67	90·60	93·44
Manganese	...	...	...	...	...	0·03
Magnesium	...	...	...	...	...	0·03

Steel fuze cap.		Zinc fuze body.		Zinc fuze body.
Fuze	L.K.Z. 16 m.V.	E.K.Z. 17.		L.K.Z. 11 Gr.
Manufacture	1916.	A.E.G. 1917.		Sb. 1917.
Iron	98·81	Zinc	90·7	91·42
Carbon	0·36	Copper	4·8	4·26
Silicon	0·06	Aluminium	3·3	3·03
Sulphur	0·05	Iron	trace	0·21
Phosphorus	0·03	Lead	1·1	1·08
Manganese	0·69	Tin	0·1	...

PERCUSSION FUZES.

Designation.—*3·7 cm. Gr. Z.* = *3·7 cm. Granat-Zünder* (fuze for 3·7 cm. H.E. shell).

Used with.—

Gun.	Pattern of Shell.	Maximum range, percussion.
3·7 cm revolver gun ...	Common shell	yards. 3,280

Nature.—Percussion : non-delay action only.

Material.—Brass.

Remarks.—It is stated in a German document that the maximum effective range of this gun against tanks is from 660 to 880 yards.
Recent specimens of this fuze bear no marking.

3·7 cm. Gr. Z.

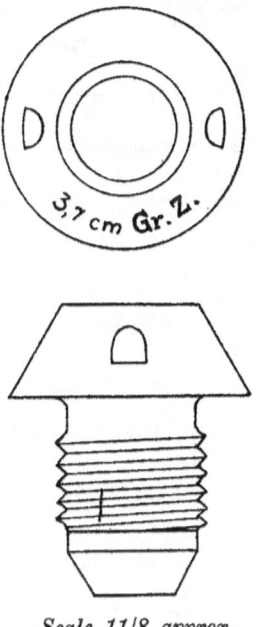

Scale 11/8 approx.

Designation.—*5 cm. Gr. Z.* = *5 cm. Granat - Zünder* (fuze for 5 cm. H.E. shell).

Used with.—

Gun.	Pattern of Shell.	Maximum range, percussion.
5 cm. gun on shielded mounting	Common shell	yards. 3,280

Nature.—Percussion : non-delay action only.

Material.—Brass.

Remarks.—This fuze arms in the bore.

It is stated in a German document that the maximum effective range of this gun against tanks is about 1,100 yards.

23

5 cm. Gr. Z.

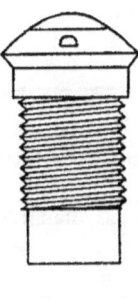

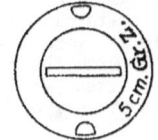

Scale 9/10 approx.

Designation.—*K.Z. 14 n.A. = Kanonen-Zünder, 1914, neuer Art* (new design of 1914 pattern gun fuze).

Used with.—

Gun.	Pattern of Shell.	Maximum range, percussion.
(7·7 cm.) field gun (96 n/A.)	'14 H.E. ... ... '15 H.E. and long gas shell (green cross)	yards. 9,186* 9,186
(7·62 cm.) infantry gun (converted Russian field gun)	H.E. shell...	1,968

Nature.—Percussion: non-delay action only.

Material.—Zinc body and steel cap. The original K.Z. 14 fuze (*see* Remarks) is made of brass, aluminium, or zinc, with either a brass or a steel cap.

Remarks.—This fuze has largely replaced the original **K.Z. 14** fuze (non-delay percussion), which was introduced towards the end of 1914 at the same time as the 1914 pattern field gun shell, and was liable to cause prematures in the bore. The K.Z. 14 fuze is, however, still used for long gas shell (green cross). The K.Z. 14 n.A. fuze differs internally from the K.Z. 14 fuze in that the safety powder pellet is in a brass sleeve; externally, it differs only in the marking and in the shape of the cap, which is more pointed.

Another variation of the K.Z. 14 fuze, marked **K.Z. 14 m.V.**, was formerly used with the 7·7 cm. long shell, but has been replaced by the pointed fuze L.K.Z. 16 m.V. It was a delay action percussion fuze designed for ricochet fire.

K.Z. 14 fuzes were often found marked **K.Z. 14 Z., K.Z. 14 Zl., K.Z. 14 Zp.,** and **K.Z. 14 Zw.**, and a **K.Z. 14 n.A. Zl.** is also found. The abbreviations **Z., Zl., Zp.** and **Zw.** probably refer to the zinc alloy (*Zinklegierung, &c.*) of which these fuzes are made, but this is not certain.

⊙ or ✡ stamped on the head of a K.Z. 14 fuze indicates a detonator of superior quality.

---

* With normal charge; the maximum range with reduced charge is 6,562 yards.

K.Z.14 n.A.

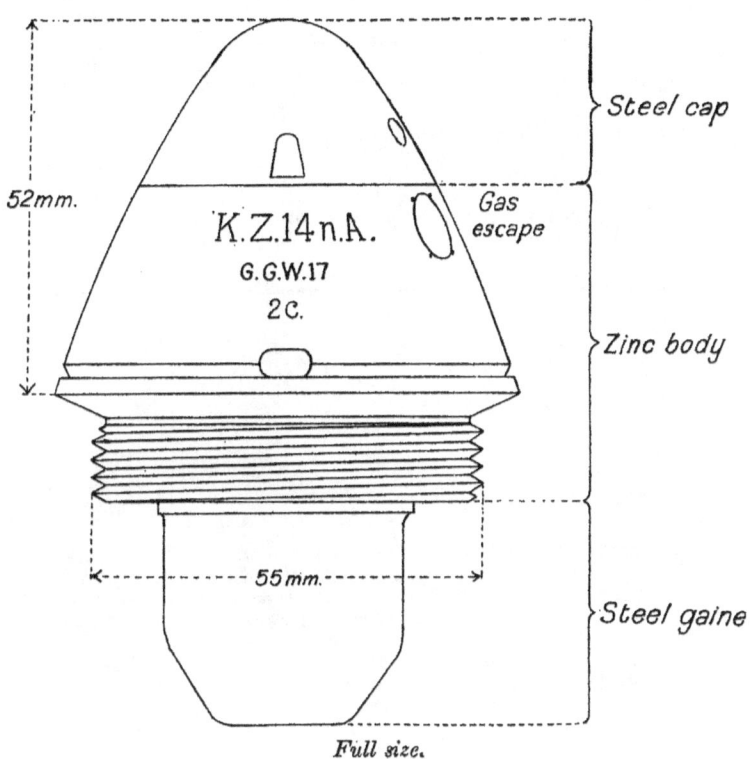

Full size.

Designation.— *L.K.Z. 16* = *Langer Kanonen - Zünder 1916* (1916 pattern long gun fuze).

Used with—

Gun.	Pattern of Shell.	Maximum range, percussion.
		yards.
(7·7 cm.) field gun (96 n/A.)	'15 H.E.	9,186
	Long H.E.	8,202
(7·7 cm.) field gun '16	'15 H.E.	10,389*
	Long H.E.	10,171*
(7·62 cm.) infantry gun (converted Russian field gun)	7·62 cm. H.E. shell	1,968

Nature.—Percussion.

Remarks.—Non-delay action fuzes are marked **L.K.Z.16 o.V.** (*o. V.* = *ohne Verzögerung*, i.e., without delay). Delay action fuzes are marked **L.K.Z. 16 m.V.** (*m. V.* = *mit Verzögerung*, i.e., with delay).

The non-delay action fuze has been superseded by the instantaneous fuzes, E.K.Z.16 and E.K.Z.17 (*see* pages 30 and 34).

The fuze proper is placed in a pointed, mild steel cap, designed for penetrative effect and increased range.

---

* With super-charge; the maximum ranges with normal charge are 9,405 and 9,296 yards respectively.

L.K.Z.16 o.V.
L.K.Z.16 m.V.

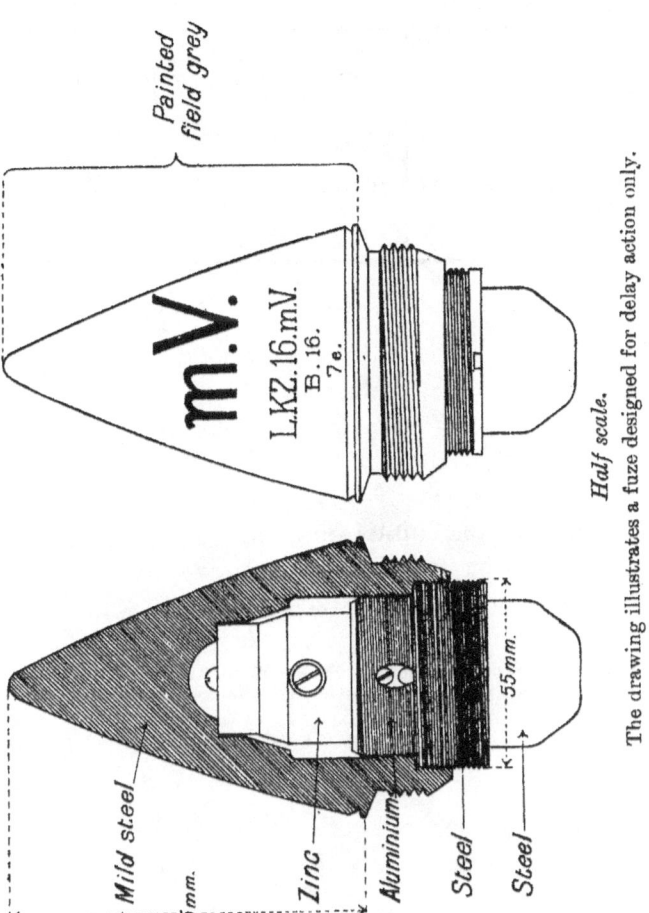

Half scale.

The drawing illustrates a fuze designed for delay action only.

Designation.— *K.Z. 16 m.V. = Kanonen-Zünder 1916 mit Verzögerung* (1916 pattern delay action gun fuze).

Used with.—

Gun.	Pattern of Shell.	Maximum range, percussion.
(7·7 cm.) field gun (96 n/A.)	'15 H.E.	yards. 9,186

Nature.—Percussion : delay action only.

Material.—Mild steel, painted grey.

Remarks.—The fuze proper is placed in a cap of mild steel. This fuze has been superseded by the L.K.Z.16 m.V. fuze (*see* page 26).

K.Z.16 m.V.

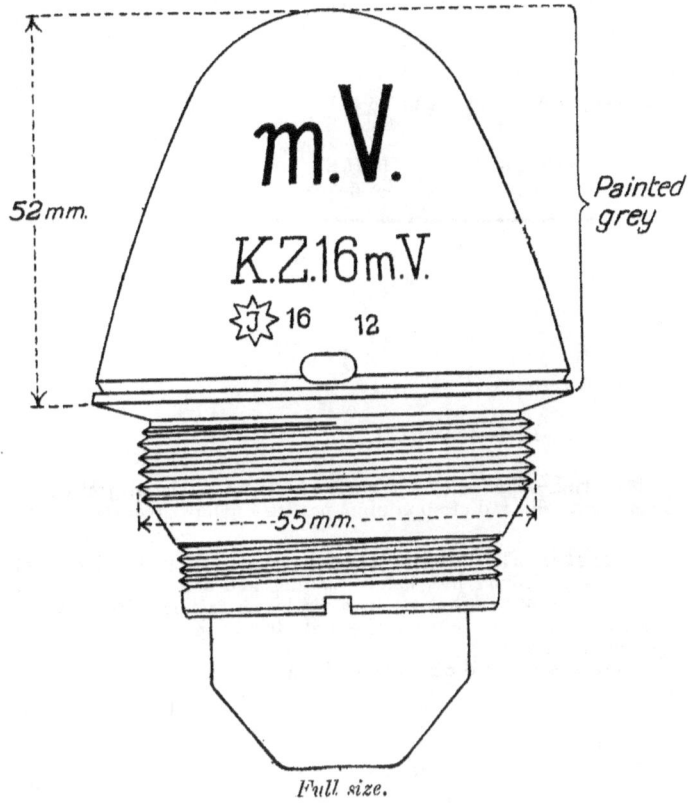

Full size.

Designation.—*E.K.Z. 16 = Empfindlicher Kanonen-Zünder 16* (1916 pattern sensitive, *i.e.*, instantaneous, gun fuze).

Used with.—

Gun.	Pattern of Shell.	Maximum range, percussion.
(7·7 cm.) field gun (96 n/A.)	'15 H.E. ... ... Long H.E. and gas shell (blue cross)	yards. 9,186 8,202
(7·7 cm.) field gun '16 ...	'15 H.E. ... ... Long H.E....	10,389* 10,171*

Nature.—Instantaneous.

Material.—Zinc alloy and steel, or all steel. The projecting rod is either a solid rod of aluminium or else a hollow steel rod.

Remarks.—This fuze is issued closed at the top by a lead seal, which is pulled off just before loading and a short rod inserted. This rod projects about an inch, its lower extremity fits into the needle holder; on impact, the rod drives the needle into the percussion cap.

A cross is stamped on fuzes used with gas shell.

---

* With super-charge; the maximum ranges with normal charge are 9,405 and 9,296 yards respectively.

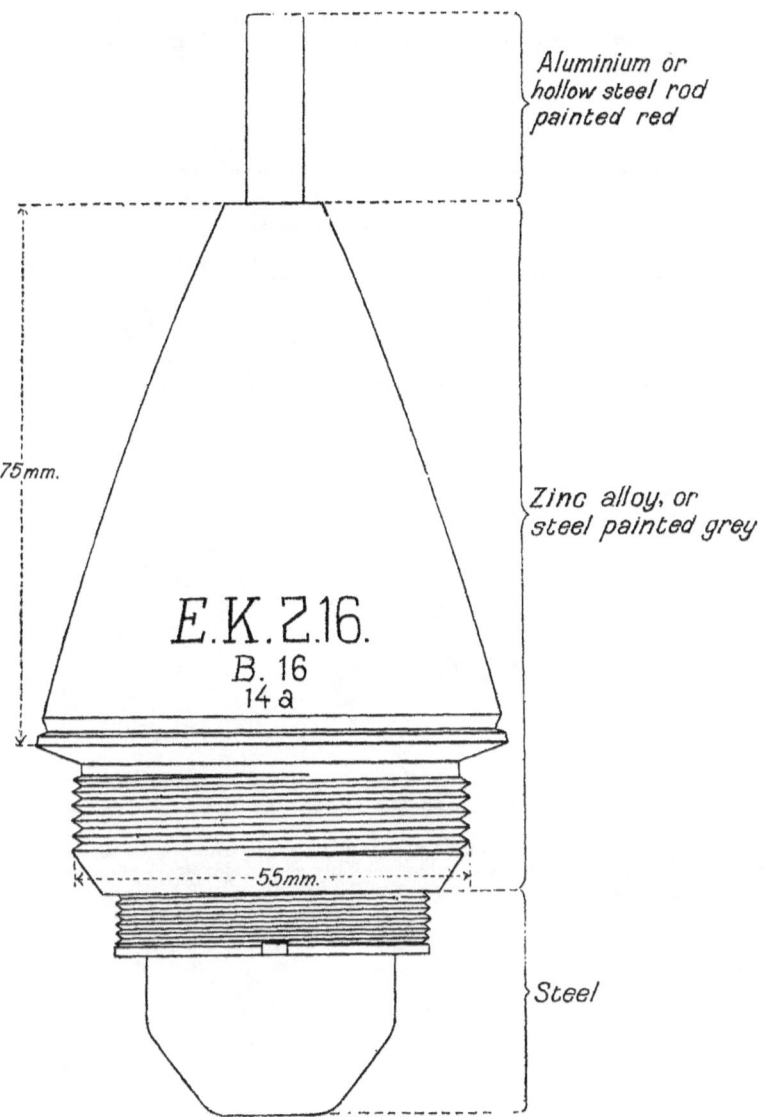

Designation.—*E.K.Z. 16 C.* = *Empfindlicher Kanonen-Zünder 16 C.* (1916 pattern sensitive, *i.e.*, instantaneous, gun fuze for "C" shell).

Used with—

Gun.	Pattern of Shell.	Maximum range, percussion.
(7·7 cm.) field gun '16 ...	"C" shell	yards. 11,264

Nature.—Instantaneous.

Material.—

Remarks.—The "C" shell is a stream-line H.E. shell, painted grey.

The **E.K.Z. 16 C.** fuze is apparently of the same type as the E.K.Z. 16 (*see* page 30), but is possibly more elongated than the latter.

E.K.Z. 16 C.

Designation.—*E.K.Z. 17 = Empfindlicher Kanonen-Zünder, 1917* 1917 pattern sensitive, *i.e.*, instantaneous, gun fuze).

Used with.—

Gun.	Pattern of Shell.	Maximum range, percussion.
		yards.
(7·7 cm.) field gun (96 n/A.)	'14 H.E.	9,186*
	'15 H.E.	9,186
	Long gas shell (yellow and green cross)	8,202
(7·7 cm.) field gun '16 ...	Long gas shell (yellow and green cross)	10,171

Nature.—Instantaneous, with centrifugal safety device.

Material.—Zinc alloy and cast-iron. In some specimens, cap and body are in one piece and of zinc alloy. The projecting rod is either a solid rod of aluminium or else a hollow steel rod.

Remarks.—This fuze is issued closed at the top by a lead seal, which is pulled off just before loading and a short rod inserted. This rod projects about an inch; its lower extremity fits into the needle holder; on impact, the rod drives the needle into the percussion cap.

A cross is stamped on fuzes used with gas shell.

When used with yellow cross gas shell, this fuze is painted green, or possibly green and black; when used with the 1914 pattern H.E. shell, it is painted black.

---

* With normal charge; the maximum range with reduced charge is 6,562 yards.

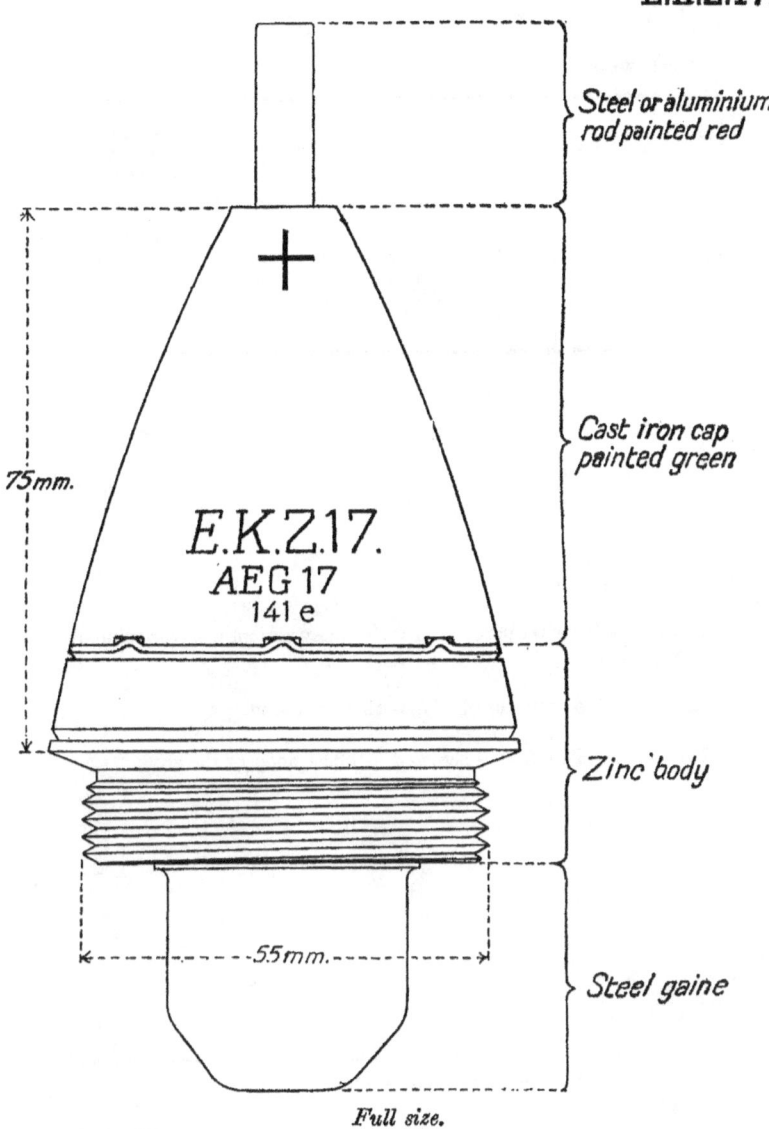

Full size.

Designation.—(?)

Used with.—

Gun.	Pattern of Shell.	Maximum range, percussion.
(7·7 cm.) field gun (96 n/A.)	Anti-tank shell with armour-piercing head (*K. Gr. 15 m.P.*)	yards. ?*

Nature.—Internal percussion fuze, delay action, with centrifugal safety device.

Material.—Aluminium body, with steel gaine.

Remarks.—This fuze is screwed into the body of the shell.

---

* Fired at short ranges with open sights.

Anti-Tank Fuze.

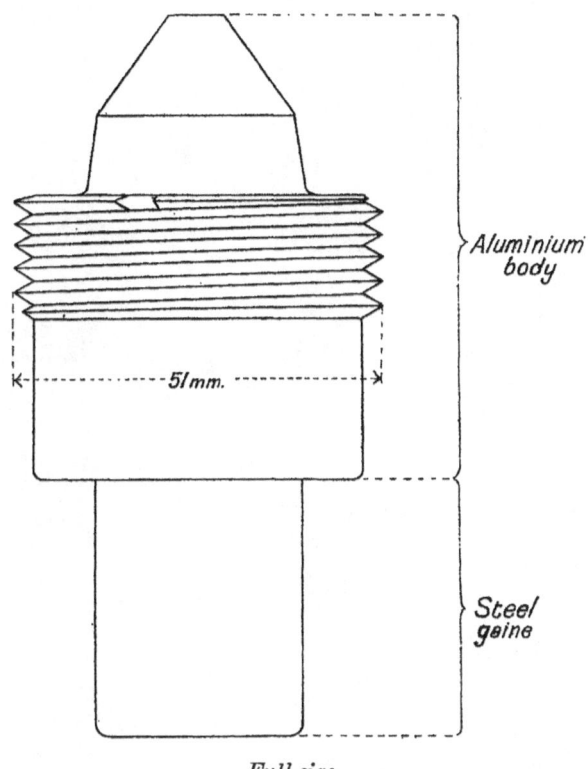

Full size.

39

40

Designation.—*H.Z.14 Fliehb.* or *H.Z.14 Fb.* = *Haubitz-Zünder, 1914, Fliehbolzen* (1914 pattern howitzer fuze with centrifugal safety bolt).

Used with.—

Gun.	Pattern of Shell.	Maximum range, percussion.
		yards.
(10·5 cm.) light field howitzer '98/'09	'14 and '15 H.E.	7,655*
	Long gas shell (green cross)§	7,655‖
(10·5 cm.) light field howitzer '16	'15 H.E.	9,186†
	Long gas shell (green cross)	9,077‖
(10·5 cm.) light field howitzer, Krupp	'15 H.E.	9,733‡
	Long gas shell (green cross)	9,624‖

Nature.—Percussion : non-delay action only.

Material.—Zinc or brass body, steel cap.

Remarks.—This fuze has largely replaced the original **H.Z. 14** fuze, which was introduced towards the end of 1914 together with the 1914 pattern light field howitzer H.E. shell, and was considered liable to cause prematures in the bore. The **H.Z. 14** fuze is, however, still used with gas shell (green cross).

The H.Z. 14 Fb. fuze differs internally from the H.Z. 14 fuze by the addition of a centrifugal safety bolt (*Fliehbolzen*). Externally, it differs only in the marking.

A red cap and ☉ or ⚔ stamped on the head of an H.Z. 14 Fb. fuze indicate a detonator of superior quality.

When used with green cross gas shell, the cap is painted green.

The H.Z. 14 fuze was also made with a deep groove round the body just below the steel cap, similar to that shown on H.Z. 14 Vorst. Fliehb. on page 47.

---

* With Charge No. 8; the usual maximum range is 6,890 yards with Charge No. 7.
† With Charge No. 9 ; the usual maximum range is 6,999 yards with Charge No. 8.
‡ With Charge No. 10 ; the usual maximum range is 6,452 yards with Charge No. 8.
§ The original H.Z.14 fuze is apparently still used with this shell.
‖ With Charges Nos. 8, 9 and 10, respectively, but it is laid down in a German document that the ranges of 6,616, 7,163 and 8,421 yards, respectively, should not be exceeded.

H.Z.14Fb.

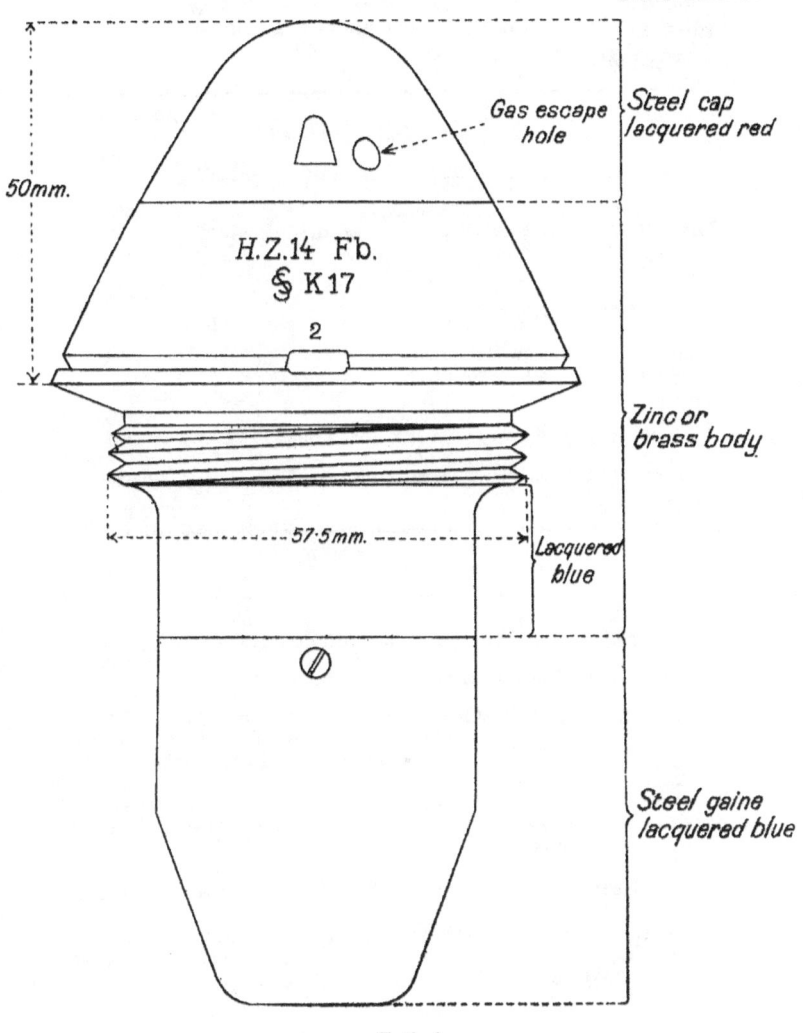

Full size.

Designation.—*H.Z. 14 Vorst. Fliehb.* or *H.Z. 14 Vorst. Fb.* = *Haubitz-Zünder, 1914, mit Vorstecker und Fliehbolzen* (1914 pattern howitzer fuze with safety pin and centrifugal bolt).

Used with.—

Gun.	Pattern of Shell.	Maximum range, percussion.
		yards.
12 cm. heavy gun	'14A H.E.	7,983
10 cm. short gun in turret	'14 and '14A H.E.	10,608
10 cm. gun with overhead shield		
10 cm. gun in turret	Ditto	11,811
10 cm. reinforced gun in turret		
10 cm. gun, 10 cm. gun '04	Ditto	11,264
10 cm. gun '14, 10 cm. gun '97	Ditto	12,085
9 cm. gun	'14A H.E.	7,109
10·67 cm. (4·2″) Russian gun	'14 H.E. for German 10 cm. gun	10,827
10·67 cm. (4·2″) Russian gun	German-made shell	10,827

Nature.—Percussion : non-delay action only.

Material.—Brass, or brass body with steel cap.

Remarks.—This fuze has replaced the original **H.Z. 14 Vorst.** fuze, from which it differs chiefly by the addition of a centrifugal safety bolt (*Fliehbolzen*). Externally, it differs only in the marking.

Fuzes have also been found with *Vrst.* and *Vst.* after the designation H Z. 14 : *Vorst.*, *Vrst.* and *Vst.* are abbreviations for *Vorstecker* (safety pin).

A red cap and ○ or ☆ stamped on the head of an H.Z. 14 Vorst. fuze indicate a detonator of superior quality.

The H.Z.14 Vorst. fuze was also made without the groove round the body just below the cap.

H.Z.14 Vorst. Fliehb.

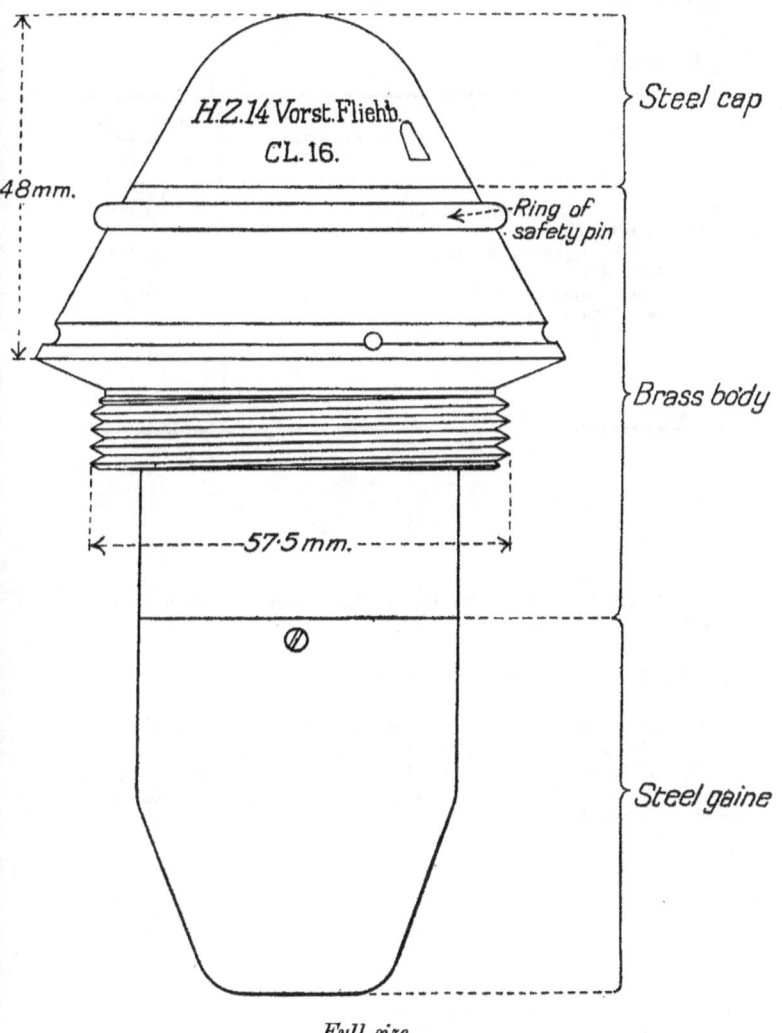

Full size.

Designation.—*H.Z. 16 = Haubitz-Zünder, 1916* (1916 pattern howitzer fuze).

Used with.—

Gun.	Pattern of Shell.	Maximum range, percussion.
(10·5 cm.) light field howitzer '98/'09	'15 and long H.E. ...	yards. 7,655*
(10·5 cm.) light field howitzer '16	Ditto	9,186*
(10·5 cm.) light field howitzer, Krupp	Ditto	9,733*

Nature.—Percussion : can be set for either non-delay or delay action.

Material.—Mild steel, painted grey.

Remarks.—According to a German document, this fuze will be replaced by the instantaneous fuze E.H.Z. 16 (*see* page 50).

This fuze is also used with 10·5 cm. blue cross gas shell, for which the maximum ranges are probably somewhat less than those given in the table above.

See first three footnotes on page 44.

H.Z.16.

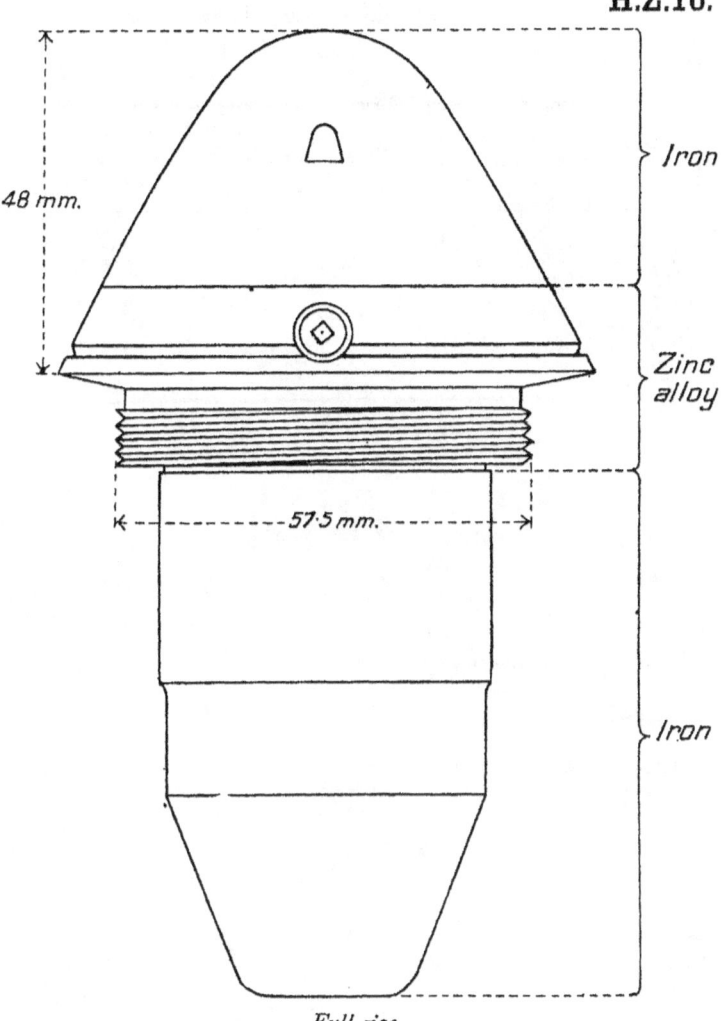

Full size.

Designation.—*E.H.Z. 16 = Empfindlicher Haubitz-Zünder, 1916* (1916 pattern sensitive, i.e., instantaneous, howitzer fuze).

Used with.—

Gun.	Pattern of Shell.	Maximum range, percussion.
(10·5 cm.) light field howitzer '98/'09	Long H.E.	yards. 7,655*
(10·5 cm.) light field howitzer '16	Ditto	9,186*
(10·5 cm.) light field howitzer, Krupp	Ditto	9,733*

Nature.—Instantaneous.

Material.—

Remarks.—According to a German document, this fuze will replace the H.Z. 16 fuze (*see* page 48).

---

* *See* first three footnotes on page 44.

E.H.Z.16.

Designation.—*E.H.Z.16 C = Empfindlicher Haubitz-Zünder 16 C* (1916 pattern sensitive, *i.e.*, instantaneous, howitzer fuze for "C" shell).

Used with.—

Gun.	Pattern of Shell.	Maximum range, percussion.
(10·5 cm.) light field howitzer '16	"C" shell...	yards 10,936*
(10·5 cm.) light field howitzer, Krupp	"C" shell...	11,210†

Nature.—Instantaneous.

Material.—

Remarks.—The "C" shell is a stream-line H.E. shell, painted grey.

The **E.H.Z.16 C** fuze is apparently of the same type as the E.H.Z.16 (*see* page 50), but is possibly more elongated than the latter.

---

* With Charge No. 9, which is the only charge used with "C" shell.
† With Charge No. 10, which is the only charge used with "C" shell.

E.H.Z.16 C.

Designation. — *E.H.Z. 17 = Empfindlicher Haubitz - Zünder, 1917* (1917 pattern sensitive, *i.e.*, instantaneous, howitzer fuze).

Used with.—

Gun.	Pattern of Shell.	Maximum range, percussion.
		yards.
(10·5 cm.) light field howitzer '98/'09	'15 H.E.	7,655*
(10·5 cm.) light field howitzer '16	Ditto	9,186*
(10·5 cm.) light field howitzer, Krupp	Ditto	9,733*

Nature.—Instantaneous, with centrifugal safety device.

Material.—Zinc alloy; the projecting rod is hollow and made of steel.

Remarks.—This fuze is issued closed at the top by a lead seal, which is pulled off just before loading and a short rod inserted. This rod projects about an inch; its lower extremity fits into the needle holder; on impact, the rod drives the needle into the percussion cap.

A cross is stamped on fuzes used with gas shell.

This fuze is also used with 10·5 cm. yellow cross gas shell, for which the maximum ranges are probably somewhat less than those given in the table above.

When used with yellow cross gas shell, this fuze is painted green, or possibly black and green. When used with the 1915 pattern H.E. shell it is painted black.

---

* *See* first three footnotes on page 44.

E.H.Z.17.

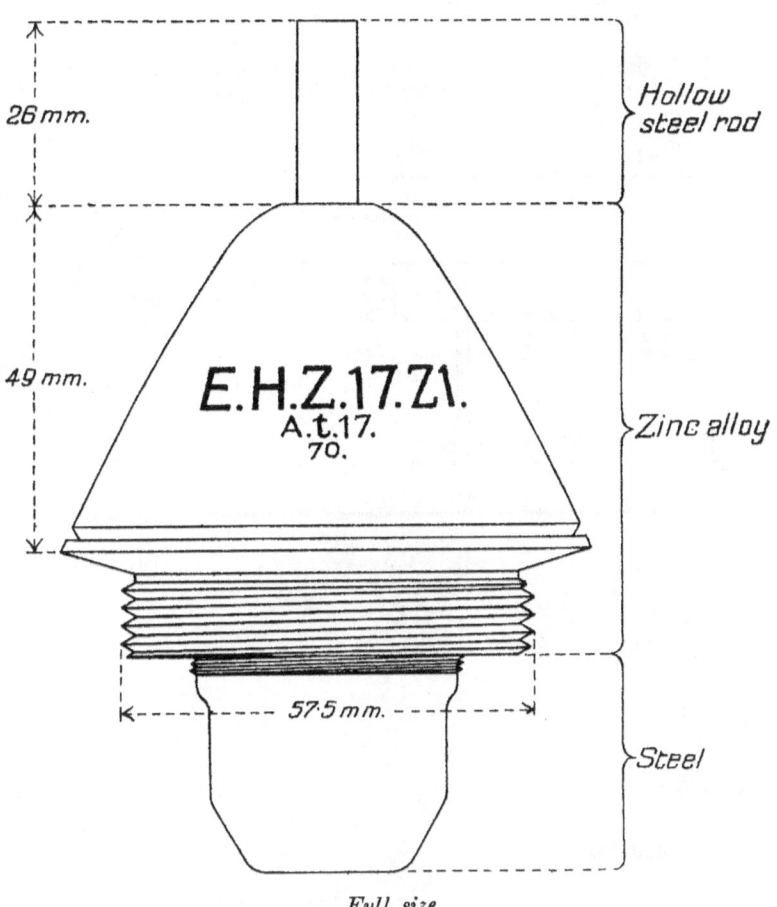

Full size.

Note.—The letters "**Zl.**" possibly refer to the zinc alloy (*Zinklegierung*) of which the fuze is made.

Designation.—*K. Z. 16 f. 10 cm. K. = Kanonen-Zünder, 1916, für 10 cm. Kanone* (1916 pattern gun fuze for 10 cm. gun).

Used with.—

Gun.	Pattern of Shell.	Maximum range, percussion.
		yards.
10 cm. short gun in turret	'14 and '14A H.E.	10,608
10 cm. gun with overhead shield		
10 cm. gun in turret	Ditto	11,811
10 cm. reinforced gun in turret		
10 cm. gun, 10 cm. gun '04	Ditto	11,264
10 cm. gun '14, 10 cm. gun '97	Ditto	12,085

Nature.—Percussion.

Material.—

Remarks.—

K.Z.16 f.10 cm. K.

Designation.—*Gr. Z. C/82 = Granat-Zünder, Construction 1882* (1882 pattern fuze for H.E. shell).

Used with.—

Gun.	Pattern of Shell.	Maximum range, percussion.
		yards.
21 cm. howitzer in turret...	'80 common	8,749
15 cm. heavy field howitzer for coast defence	'88 H.E.	6,616
(15 cm.) heavy field howitzer	'88, '14 and '14A H.E. and incendiary " C "	6,616
(15 cm.) heavy field howitzer '02	'88, '14 and '14A H.E. ...	8,147
	Incendiary " C "	7,109
(15 cm.) heavy field howitzer '13	'14 and '14A H.E. ...	9,296
	Incendiary " C "	8,749
	'88 H.E.	8,147
15 cm. long gun with chase rings	'14 and '14A H.E. with forward driving band	8,749
	'80 common shell... ...	
15 cm. gun with chase rings	'14 and '14A H.E. with forward driving band	8,640
	'80 common shell... ...	8,312

Nature.—Percussion : non-delay action only.

Material.—Brass.

Remarks.—This fuze arms in the bore.

There is a variety of this fuze, known as **Gr. Z. 82 (Kp.)**, in which a slight alteration is made in the interior and a steel cap is placed over the top of the fuze. The object of these variations is to prevent bursts in the bore and to reduce the probability of blinds.

Gr. Z. 82 is usually employed in connection with a fuze-hole socket or gaine (*Mundlochfutter*) and exploder (*Zündladung*). In the plate opposite, it is shown screwed into the 1880 pattern fuze-hole socket (Mdlchf. 80). When Gr. Z. 82 (Kp.) is combined with Mdlchf. 88 and Zdlg. 82, the combination is called "Granat-Zündung 88" (Gr. Zdg. 88), which is used with the 1914 and 1914A patterns of 15 cm. shell mentioned above.

Gr. Z. 82.

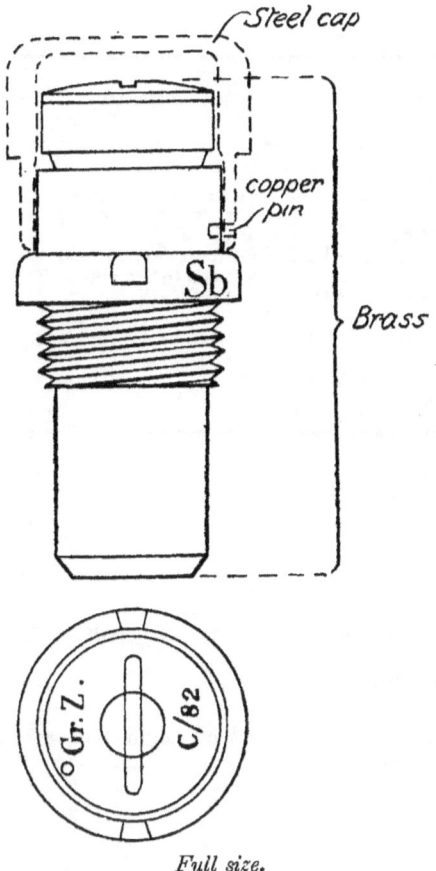

Full size.

Designation.—*Gr. Z. 92 = Granat-Zünder, 1892* (1892 pattern fuze for H.E. shell).

Used with.—

Gun.	Pattern of Shell.	Maximum range, percussion.
		yards.
21 cm. mortar	'96 type gas shell (green cross and yellow cross)	7,874 ?
"Mortar" (21 cm.) ...	Ditto	10,280 ?
(15 cm.) heavy field howitzer	H.E. (pattern?) and gas shell (green cross)	6,616
(15 cm.) heavy field howitzer '02	Ditto	8,147
(15 cm.) heavy field howitzer '13	Ditto	9,296
(15 cm.) long heavy field howitzer '13	Ditto	9,296

Nature.—Percussion : non-delay action only.

Material.—Brass.

Remarks.—This fuze is used in conjunction with an exploder in a steel or brass gaine, Zdlg. 92.

Gr. Z. 92.

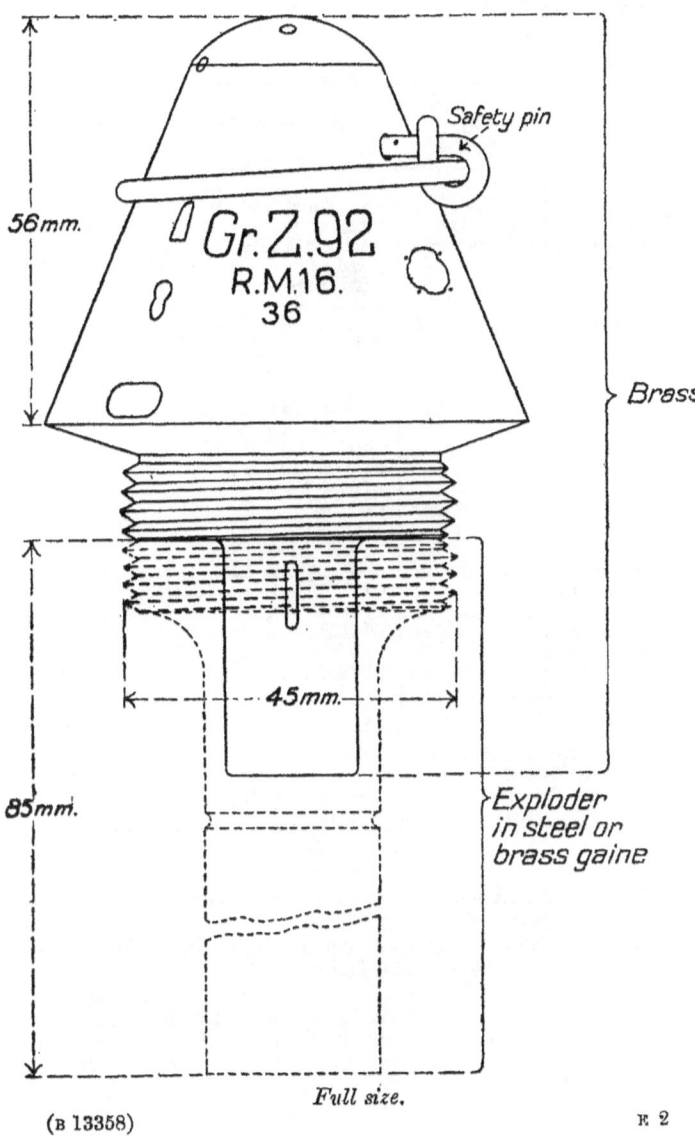

Full size.

Designation.—*Gr. Z. 04* = *Granat-Zünder, 1904* (1904 pattern fuze for H.E. shell).

Used with.—

Gun.	Pattern of Shell.	Maximum range, percussion.
		yards.
21 cm. mortar	'88, '14 and '14A, H.E.	8,968
"Mortar" (21 cm.)	Ditto	9,952
(15 cm.) heavy field howitzer	'12, '12 n/A., '14 and '14A, H.E., T, K, and green T gas shell and N smoke shell	6,616
(15 cm.) heavy field howitzer '02	Ditto	8,147
(15 cm.) heavy field howitzer '13	Ditto	9,296
(15 cm.) long heavy field howitzer '13	Ditto	9,296
15 cm. long gun with chase rings	'14 and '14A, H.E., with forward driving band	8,749
15 cm. gun with chase rings	Ditto	8,640
15 cm. long gun	'96, '12, '12 n/A., '14 and '14A, H.E.	10,936
15 cm. gun with overhead shield	'03 H.E.	17,060
15 cm. gun L/30	'12 and '12 n/A, H.E.	?
15 cm. experimental gun on wheeled carriage	'03 H.E., with false cap	21,107
	'03 H.E., ordinary pattern	18,482
13 cm. gun	'14 H.E.	15,748
10 cm. coast defence gun on wheeled carriage	'16 H.E.	16,295
10 cm. gun with overhead shield; 10 cm. gun in turret; 10 cm. reinforced gun in turret	'15 H.E.	11,811
10 cm. gun, 10 cm. gun '04	Ditto	11,264
10 cm. guns, '14 and '97	Ditto	12,085
20·3 cm. (8″) Russian howitzer	German-made shell	9,515
15·24 cm. (6″) Russian gun	German '12 H.E.	13,124

Nature.—Percussion: with or without delay action (the "delay" = 1 second, approximately).

Material.—Brass body, steel cap and steel gaine. Specimens have recently been found made of zinc alloy.

Remarks.—There is a variation of this fuze known as **Gr. Z. 04/14.** It is used with the 1914 and 1914A pattern 21 cm. shells and with the German-made shell for the 20·3 cm. (8″) Russian howitzer, and is externally identical with Gr. Z. 04, except for the designation.

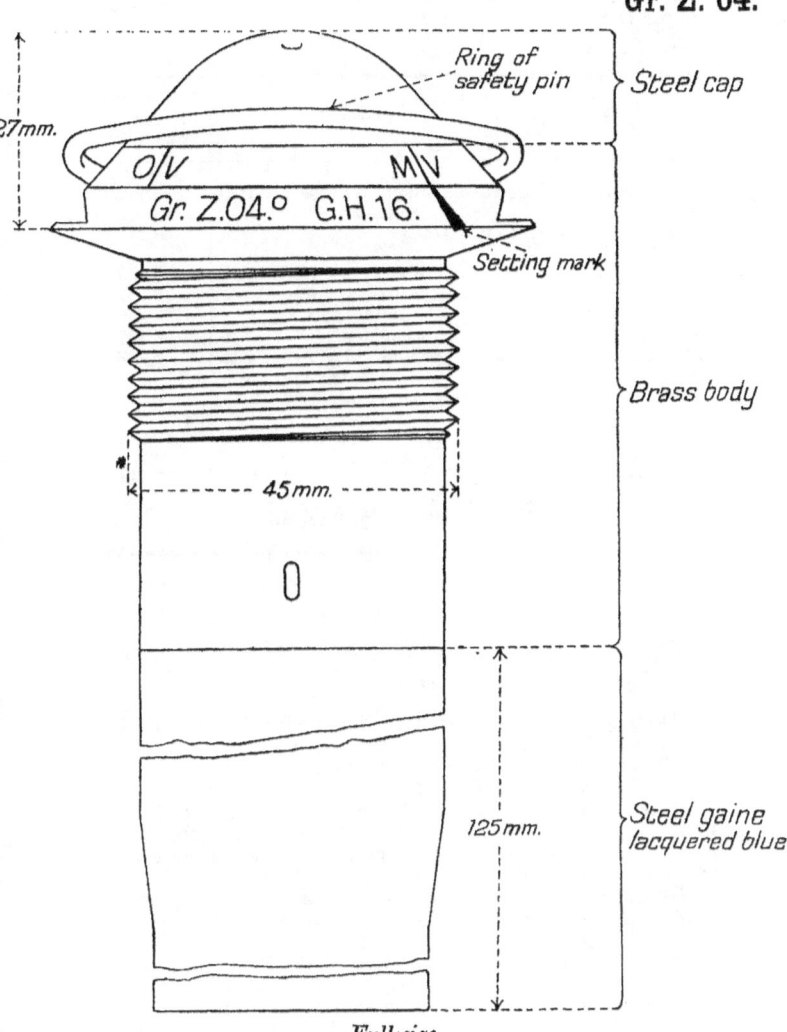

Full size.

Designation.—*Gr. Z. 14 = Granat-Zünder, 1914* (1914 pattern fuze for H.E. shell).

Used with.—

Gun.	Pattern of Shell.	Maximum range, percussion.
		yards.
(15 cm.) heavy field howitzer	'14 and '14A H.E., and incendiary "B"	6,616
(15 cm.) heavy field howitzer '02	Ditto	8,147
(15 cm.) heavy field howitzer '13	{ '14 and '14A H.E. ... { Incendiary "B" ...	9,296 8,147
(15 cm.) long heavy field howitzer '13	{ '14 and '14A H.E. ... { Incendiary "B" ...	9,296 8,147
15 cm. long gun with chase rings	'14 and '14A H.E., with forward driving band	8,749
15 cm. gun with chase rings	Ditto	8,640
15 cm. long gun	'14 and '14A H.E. ..	10,936
15 cm. gun L/30	'14 H.E.	?
12 cm. heavy gun	Ditto	7,984
9 cm. gun	Ditto	7,109
15·24 cm. (6") Russian howitzer	German-made shell ...	?

Nature.—Percussion : non-delay action only.

Material.—Brass and steel.

Remarks.—This fuze was introduced with the 1914 and 1914 A patterns of H.E. shell to meet the demand for a comparatively simply made non-delay action percussion fuze.

The following variations of this fuze have been found :—

G. Gr. Z. 14 and **Kz. Gr. Z. 14** in which "G" and "K" probably stand for "Grosser" and "Kurzer" (large and short), which possibly refer to the size of the exploder and the consequent length of the gaine (*see* page 138).

Gr. Z. 14 n.A. A variation which has taken the place of the original Gr. Z. 14 (*see* page 72).

A red cap and ◯ or ⋈ stamped on the head of this fuze indicate a detonator of superior quality.

Gr. Z. 14.

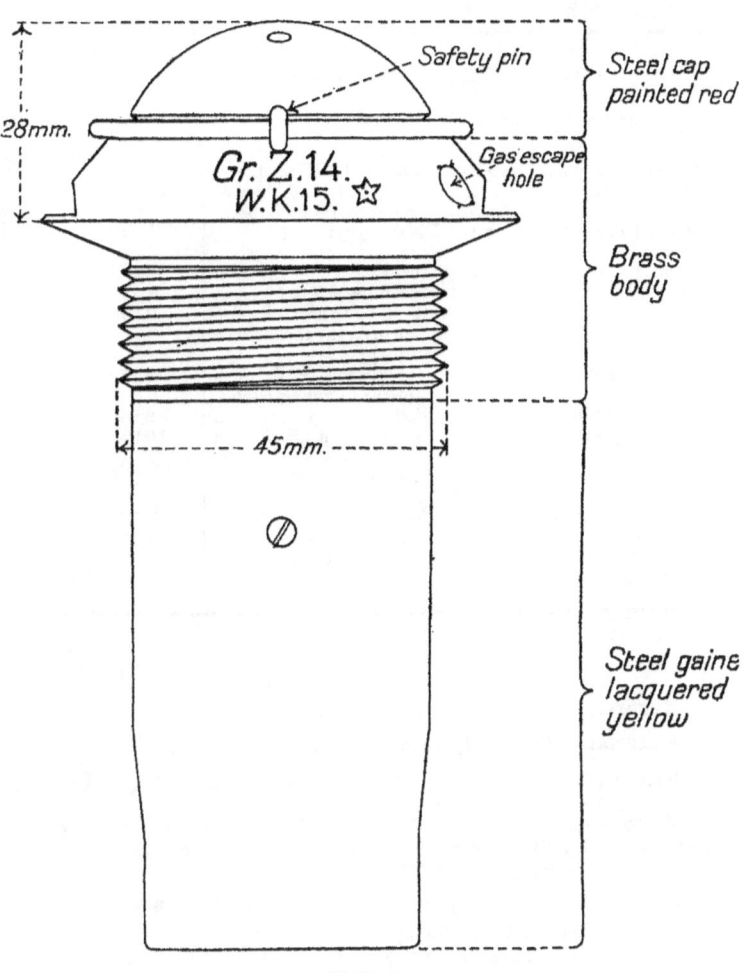

Full size.

Designation.—*Gr. Z. 14 n.A.* = *Granat-Zünder, 1914, neuer Art* (new design of 1914 pattern fuze for H.E. shell).

Used with,—

Gun.	Pattern of Shell.	Maximum range, percussion.
		yards.
(15 cm.) heavy field howitzer	'14 and '14A H.E., incendiary "B" and '12 n/A. gas shell (green cross)	6,616
(15 cm.) heavy field howitzer '02	Ditto	8,147
(15 cm.) heavy field howitzer '13	{ Ditto ... ... { Incendiary "B" ...	9,296 8,147
(15 cm.) long heavy field howitzer '13	'14 and '14A H.E. and '12 n/A. gas shell (green cross)	9,296
15 cm. long gun with chase rings	'14 and '14A H.E., with forward driving band	8,749
15 cm. gun with chase rings	Ditto	8,640
15 cm. long gun	'14 and '14A H.E. and '12 n/A. gas shell (green cross)	10,936
15 cm. gun L/30	'14 H.E.	?
12 cm. heavy gun	Ditto	7,984
9 cm. gun	Ditto	7,109
15·24 cm. (6") Russian howitzer	German-made shell ...	?

Nature.—Percussion : non-delay action only.

Material.—Brass body with steel cap and steel gaine.

Remarks.—A steel cover is fastened over the projecting conical portion by two screws.

When used with gas shell, there is no set screw to hold the gaine, but the joint between the gaine and the shell is sealed with cement of the magnesium oxychloride type.

A red cap and ○ or ☆ stamped on the head of a Gr.Z. 14 n.A. fuze indicate a detonator of superior quality.

A green cap and a yellow cover denote a "Green Cross" gas shell (15 cm.).

The whole fuze is sometimes painted yellow when used with H.E. shell.

Gr. Z. 14 n.A.

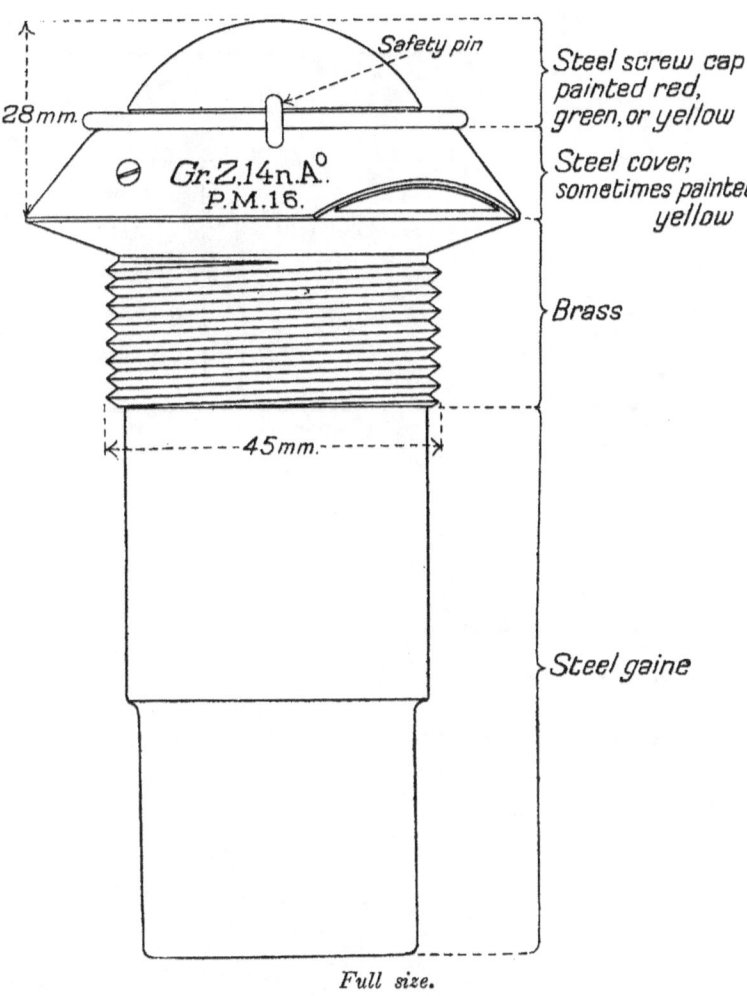

- 28 mm.
- Safety pin
- Gr.Z.14n.A°. P.M.16.
- 45 mm.
- Steel screw cap painted red, green, or yellow
- Steel cover, sometimes painted yellow
- Brass
- Steel gaine

Full size.

Designation.—*Gr. Z. 17 = Granat-Zünder, 1917* (1917 pattern fuze for H.E. shell).

Used with.—

Gun.	Pattern of Shell.	Maximum range, percussion.
		yards.
(15 cm.) heavy field howitzer	'12 n/A. and '14 H.E. ...	6,616
(15 cm.) heavy field howitzer '02	Ditto	8,147
(15 cm.) heavy field howitzer '13	Ditto	9,296
(15 cm.) long heavy field howitzer '13	Ditto	9,296

Nature.—Instantaneous.

Material.—Steel and white metal.

Remarks.—This fuze will replace the Gr. Z. 14 n.A. fuze (*see* page 72).

Gr. Z. 17.

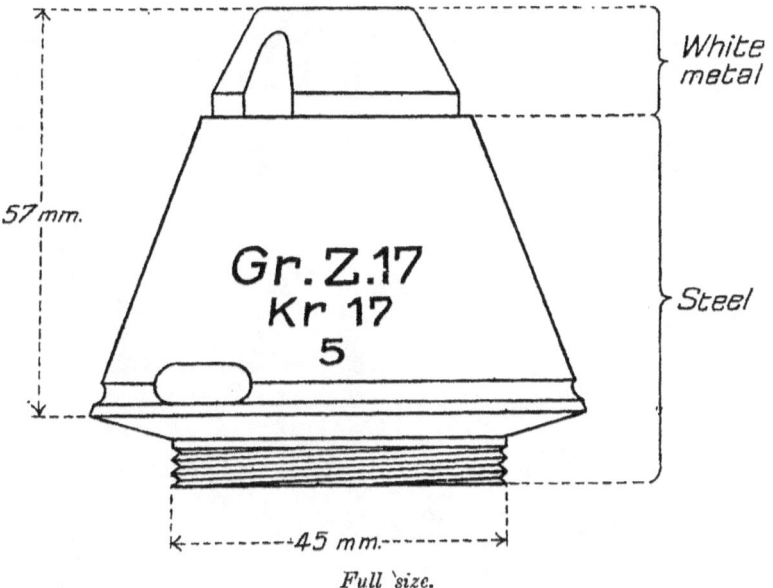

Full size.

The above is only an approximate sketch made from a fired specimen.

Designation.—*lg. Bd. Z. 10* = *langer Boden-Zünder, 1910* (long 1910 pattern base fuze).

Used with.—

Gun.	Pattern of Shell.	Maximum range, percussion.
		yards.
28 cm. coast defence howitzer on coast defence howitzer mounting	'06 H.E.	12,467
21 cm. bronze coast defence mortar	Ditto	8,530
"Mortar" (21 cm.) ...	'96 (converted) H.E. ...	10,280
21 cm. gun with chase rings	'06 H.E.	10,718
15 cm. gun on coast defence mounting, '07	Ditto	8,530
15 cm. gun with overhead shield	'06 H.E.	17,060
13 cm. gun	13 cm. H.E. and incendiary	15,748

Nature.—Percussion: non-delay, short delay or long delay action (*vide* O.V., 1 V and 2 V on the plate).

Material.—Brass.

Remarks.—With the 1906 pattern shell for 28 cm. howitzer, the fuze is set without delay action (O.V.) for ranges below 4,100 m. and at 2 V for ranges above 4,100 m.

A variation of this fuze has been found fitted to a 13 cm. incendiary shell. Above the designation lg. Bd. Z. 10 are the words Brd. Gesch. = *Brand-Geschoss*, implying that it is designed for use with incendiary shell. The fuze is otherwise externally identical with the ordinary lg. Bd. Z. 10 fuze.

This fuze has superseded an older pattern called **Bd. Z. 06** (*see* page 138).

lg. Bd. Z. 10.

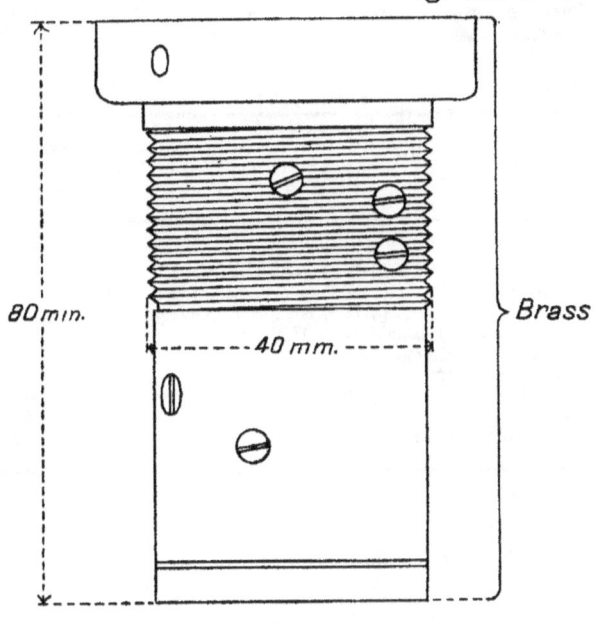

80 min. — 40 mm. — Brass

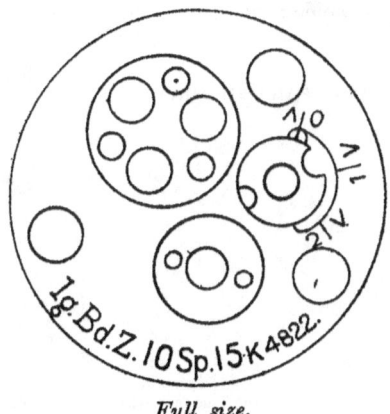

Full size.

Designation.—*kz. Bd. Z. 10 = kurzer Boden-Zünder, 1910* (short 1910 pattern base fuze).

Used with.—

Gun.	Pattern of Shell.	Maximum range, percussion.
		yards.
42 cm. howitzer	H.E. with false cap H.E. with diaphragm H.E. without diaphragm...	approx. 18,000
28 cm. coast defence howitzer on coast defence howitzer mounting	Long H.E.	10,608
21 cm. mortar	'96 n/A.H.E.	7,874
"Mortar" (21 cm.)	Ditto	10,280
10 cm. coast defence gun*...	'06 H.E.	11,264

Nature.—Percussion: non-delay, short delay or long delay action (*vide* O.V., 1 V and 2 V on the plate).

Material.—Brass, with steel gaine.

Remarks.—

---

* When used with this gun, the fuze is marked **kz.Bd. Z. 10 Kst.K.**

kz. Bd. Z. 10.

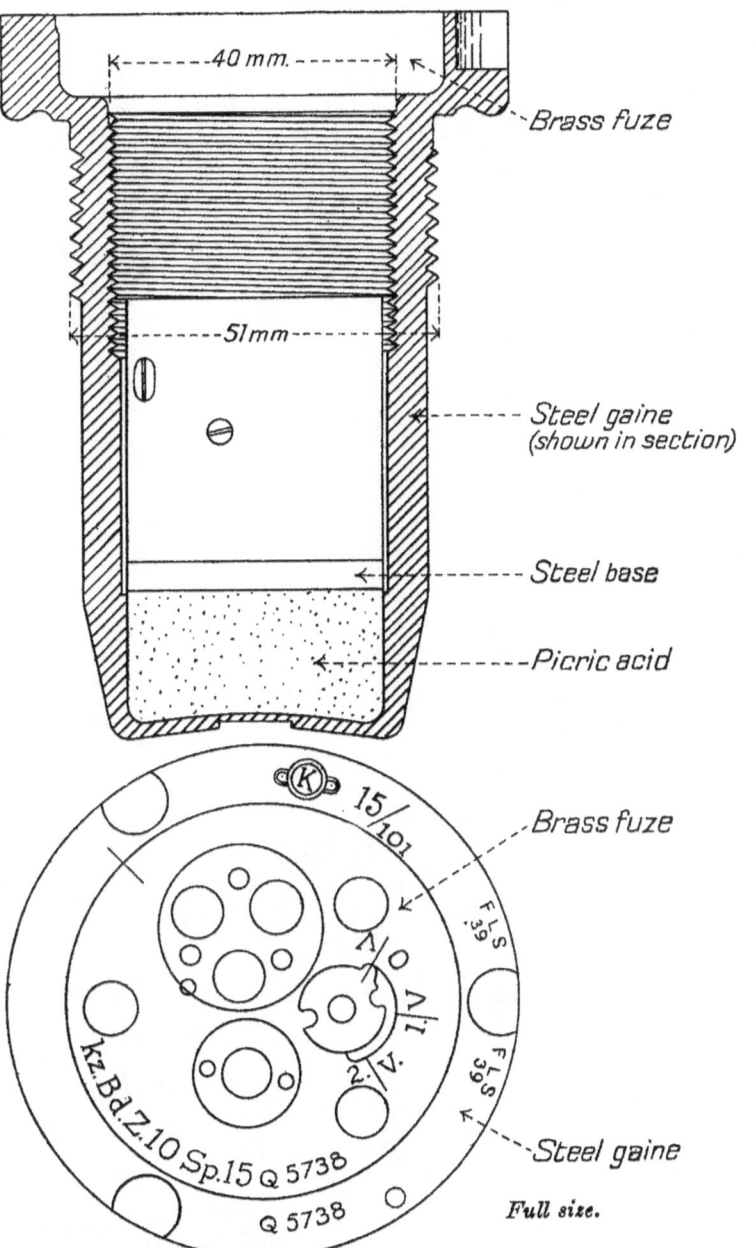

Full size.

TIME AND PERCUSSION FUZES.

Designation.—*Dopp. Z. 96 n/A.* = *Doppel-Zünder, 1896, neuer Art* (new design of 1896 pattern time and percussion fuze).

Used with.—

Gun.	Pattern of Shell.	Maximum range.	
		Time.	Perc'n.
(7·7 cm.) field gun (96 n/A.)	'96 shrapnel (converted)	yards. 7,655*	yards. 9,186
(7·7 cm.) field gun '16 ...	Ditto	8,421†	8,968†

Nature.—Time and percussion.

Graduations.—Graduated originally from 2 to 53½, then from 2 to 65, and in fuzes of recent manufacture from 6 to 70 (lowest and highest figures are 6 and 70) in hundreds of metres (50 = 5,000 metres); each of the smallest divisions is equivalent to 50 metres of range.

When the setting mark is opposite the cross on the disc covering the gas escape, the fuze is set for percussion.

The fuze is set at K when the shell is intended for use as case shot (this K is sometimes omitted).

Material.—Aluminium, with cap of brass or steel.

---

* Fuzes have been found graduated up to 7,150 metres (7,820 yards).
† With normal charge; the super-charge is apparently not used with shrapnel.

Dopp. Z. 96 n/A.

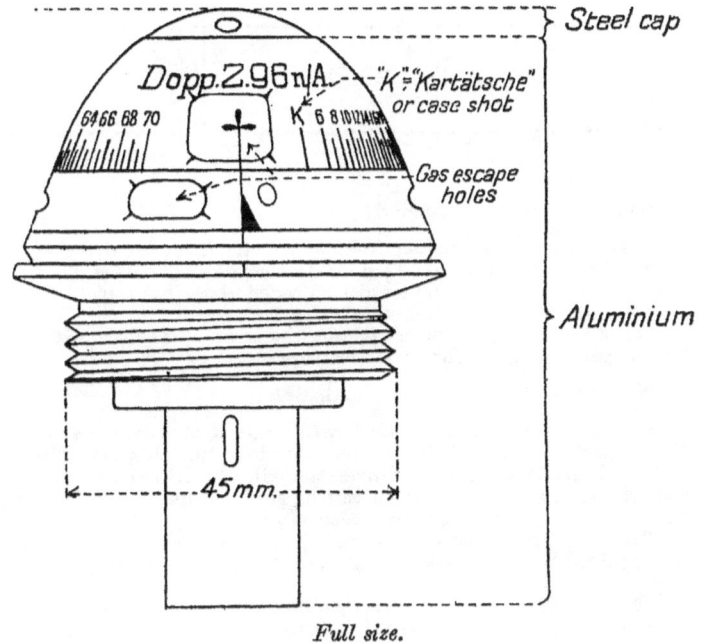

Full size.

Designation.—*K.Z. 11 Gr.= Kanonen-Zünder, 1911, Granate* (1911 pattern gun fuze for H.E. shell).

Used with.—

Gun.	Pattern of Shell.	Maximum range.	
		Time.	Perc'n.
(7·7 cm.) field gun (96 n/A.)	'15 H.E.	yards. 7,874	yards 9,186

Nature.—Time and percussion.

Graduations.—Graduated from 2 or 4 to 72 in hundreds of metres (72 = 7,200 metres): each of the smallest divisions from 2 to 15 is equivalent to 100 metres of range, those from 15 to 72 are equivalent to 50 metres.

When the setting mark is opposite the cross on the disc covering the gas escape, the fuze is set for percussion.

Material.—Aluminium alloy and steel.

Remarks.—This fuze is used principally against aeroplanes. It is a modification of **K.Z. 11**, introduced in 1916, for use with H.E. shell, but not with the universal shell. It differs externally from the K.Z. 11 fuze in that the setting stud, the marks " G " and " S," and the corrector scale are omitted.

The most recent pattern of this fuze is sometimes marked **K.Z. 11 Gr. l.B.**, or the letters "l.B." are stamped elsewhere on the fuze.

The cap of the K.Z. 11 Gr. fuze, when used with the 1915 pattern 7·7 cm. H.E. shell issued to anti-aircraft guns, is painted yellow.

A variation of this fuze is marked **K.Z. 11 Gr.** $\frac{nur}{Bz.}$ and is a time fuze only, with no percussion action. It has presumably been introduced for use with H.E. shell fired from anti-aircraft guns. With the exception of the additional "nur Bz." (*nur Brennzünder*, or time fuze only) in the designation and the fact that the cap is distinctly less pointed, it is externally identical with K.Z. 11 Gr.

The K.Z. 11 Gr. fuze has been largely superseded by the L.K.Z. 11 Gr. fuze (*see* page 95).

K.Z.11Gr.

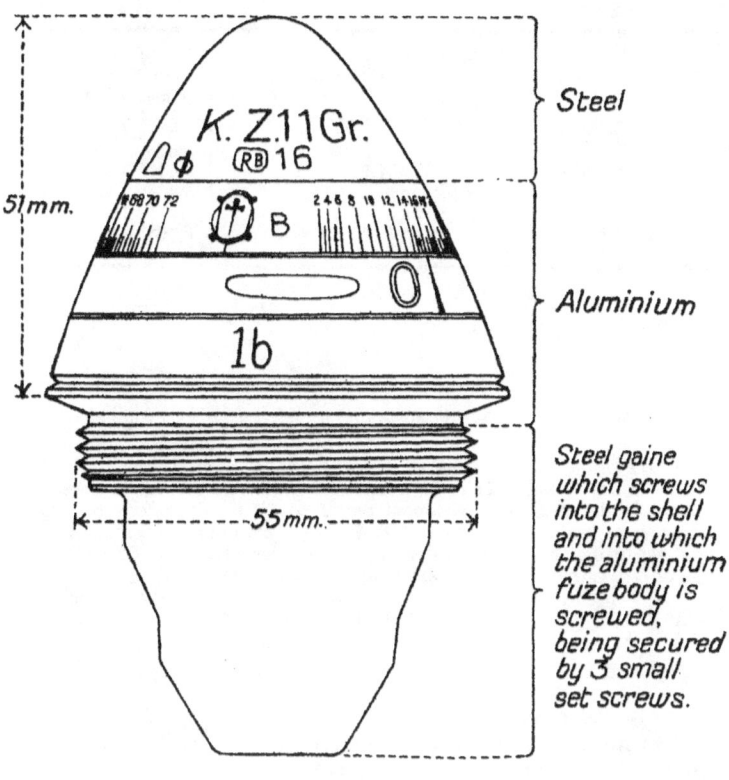

Full size.

In another variation of this fuze, the letters **O.Az.** (*ohne Aufschlagzündung* = without percussion system), are stamped on the right of the setting mark. The upper time ring is graduated in seconds from 3 to 30, and in fifths of a second from $2\frac{2}{5}$ to $30\frac{1}{5}$. Two fifths or ·4 of each second is further indicated by the figure 4. The cap is painted red. This fuze is used with the H.E. shell, of German manufacture, fired from the 7·62 cm. (3″) Russian field gun converted for anti-aircraft work.

Designation.—*L.K.Z. 11 Gr.* = *Langer Kanonen-Zünder, 1911, Granate* (long 1911 pattern gun fuze for H.E. shell).

Used with.—

Gun.	Pattern of Shell.	Maximum range.	
		Time.	Perc'n.
		yards.	yards.
(7·7 cm.) field gun (96 n/A.)	'15 H.E.	5,468*	9,186
	Long H.E.	5,468	8,202
(7·7 cm.) field gun '16	'15 H.E.	5,468*	10,389†

Nature.—Time and percussion.

Graduations.—Graduated from 4 to 72 (lowest and highest figures are 4 and 72) in hundreds of metres (68 = 6,800 metres). Each of the smallest divisions from 2 to 15 is equivalent to 100 metres of range, those from 15 to 72 are equivalent to 50 metres.

According to a German document, the latest pattern of this fuze is only graduated up to 5,000 metres (5,468 yards).

When the setting mark is opposite the cross on the disc covering the gas escape, the fuze is set for percussion.

Material.—Cap of zinc alloy; aluminium time rings.

Remarks.—This pointed fuze was introduced for use with the long pattern field gun shell, to replace the K.Z. 11 Gr. fuze. It does not, however, appear to be extensively used.

---

* Fuze setting, not range.
† With super-charge; the maximum range with normal charge is 9,405 yards.

L.K.Z.11Gr.

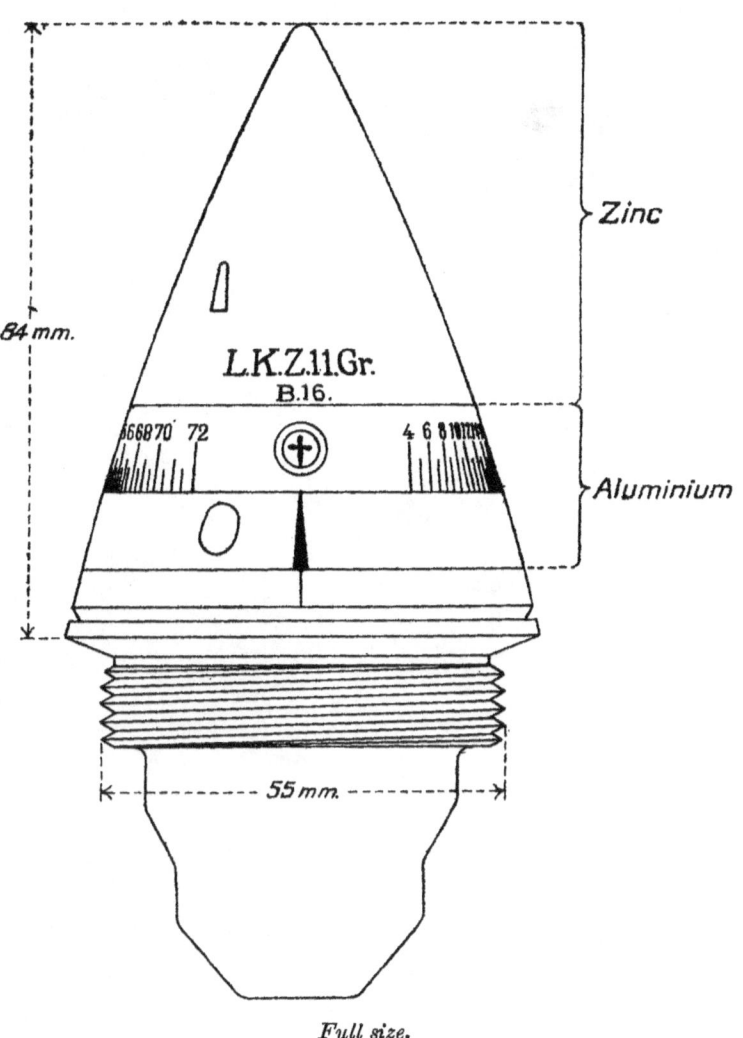

Full size.

Designation.—*H.Z. 05 Gr. l.B.* = *Haubitz-Zünder, 1905, Granate, lange Brennlänge* (1905 pattern long-burning howitzer fuze for H.E. shell).

Used with.—

| Gun. | Pattern of Shell. | Maximum range. ||
		Time.	Perc'n.
(10·5 cm.) light field howitzer '98/'09	'15 and long H.E.	yards. 5,468	yards. 7,655†
(10·5 cm.) light field howitzer '16	Ditto	5,468*	9,186†
(10·5 cm.) light field howitzer, Krupp	Ditto	5,468*	9,733†

Nature.—Time and percussion (with and without delay action).

Graduations.—Graduated from 7 to 70 (lowest and highest figures are 8 and 70) in hundreds of metres (52 = 5,200 metres); each of the smallest divisions is equivalent to 50 metres of range.

When the setting mark is opposite the cross, the fuze is set for percussion.

The original pattern of **H.Z. 05 Gr.** fuze was graduated from 7 to 53 in hundreds of metres, and a later pattern was graduated up to 63, the maximum ranges with time fuze being 5,796 and 6,890 yards, respectively. When the fuze was set to the red mark, the shell burst from 30 to 90 yards from the muzzle with shrapnel effect.

According to a German document, the latest pattern of this fuze is only graduated up to 5,000 metres (5,468 yards).

Material.—Brass body with aluminium time rings and steel cap.

Remarks.—This fuze is also used with 10·5 cm. blue cross gas shell, for which the maximum ranges are probably somewhat less than those given in the table above.

---

* Fuze-setting, not range.
† *See* first three footnotes on page 44.

H.Z.05 Gr. 1.B.

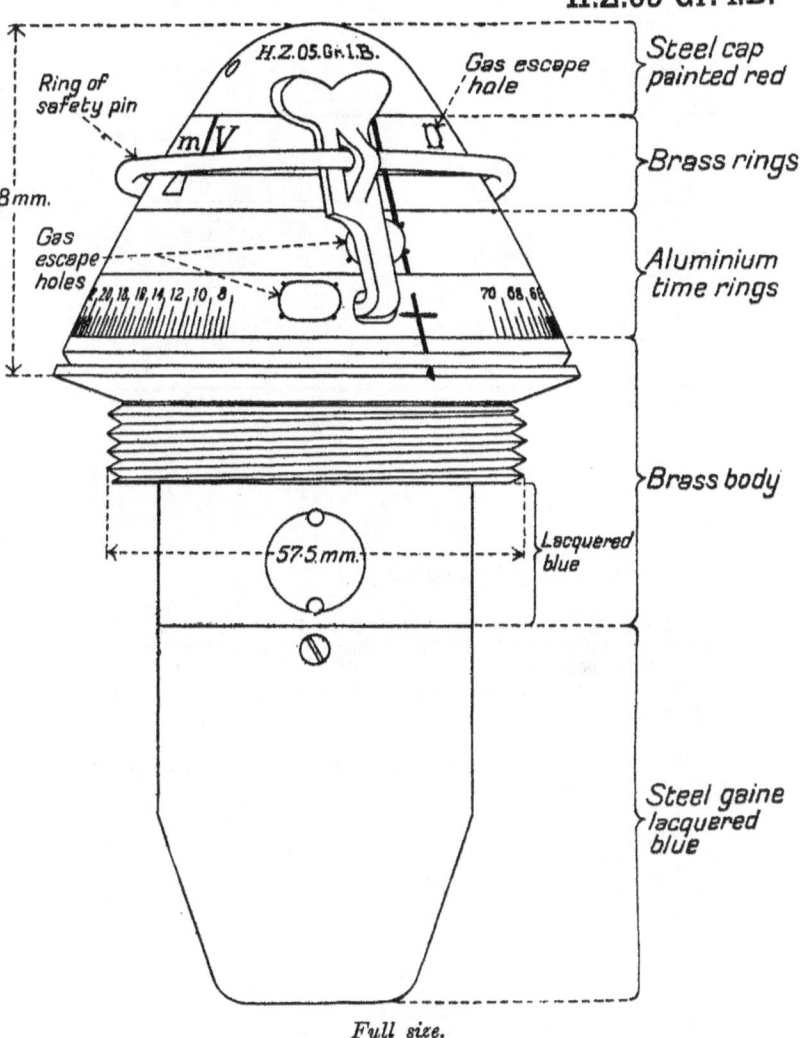

Full size.

Designation.—*H.Z. 05 Schr.* = *Haubitz-Zünder, 1905, Schrapnel* (1905 pattern howitzer fuze for shrapnel).

Used with.—

Gun.	Pattern of Shell.	Maximum range.	
		Time.	Perc'n.
		yards.	yards.
(10·5 cm.) light field howitzer '98/'09	'16 shrapnel	7,655	7,655
(10·5 cm.) light field howitzer '16	Ditto	7,655*	9,186
(10·5 cm.) light field howitzer, Krupp	Ditto	7,655*	9,733

Nature.—Time and percussion.

Graduations.—Graduated from 3 to 70 (lowest and highest figures are either 3 or 4, and 70) in hundreds and fifties of metres (68 = 6,800 metres).

When the setting mark is opposite the cross, the fuze is set for percussion.

Material.—Body usually of zinc alloy, with aluminium time rings and steel cap.

Remarks.—

---

* Fuze-setting, not range. This fuze was designed for the '98/'09 pattern light field howitzer.

H.Z.05 Schr.

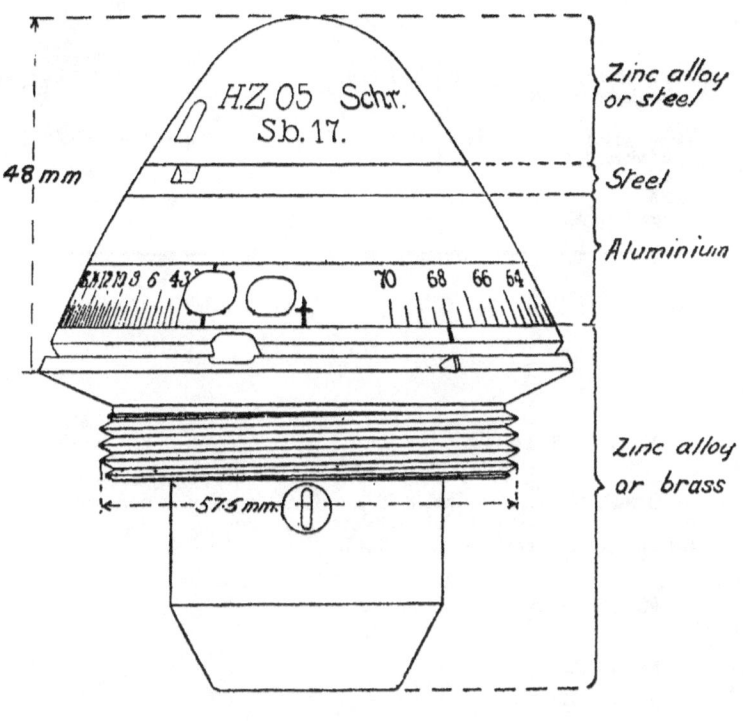

Full size.

Designation.—*Lg.Zdr.S/22 = Leuchtgeschoss-Zünder, 22 Sekunden* (star shell fuze, 22 seconds).

Used with.—

Gun.	Pattern of Shell.	Maximum range, time.
(10·5 cm.) light field howitzer '98/'09	Star shell	yards. 4,740
(10·5 cm.) light field howitzer '16	Ditto	at least 4,740
(10·5 cm.) light field howitzer, Krupp	Ditto	at least 4,740

Nature.—Time fuze.

Graduations.—Graduated from 0 to 22 in seconds and tenths of a second (lowest and highest figures are 0 and 22). From 0 to 1, the smaller graduations are omitted.

Material—Aluminium and brass.

Remarks.—

Lg. Zdr. S/22.

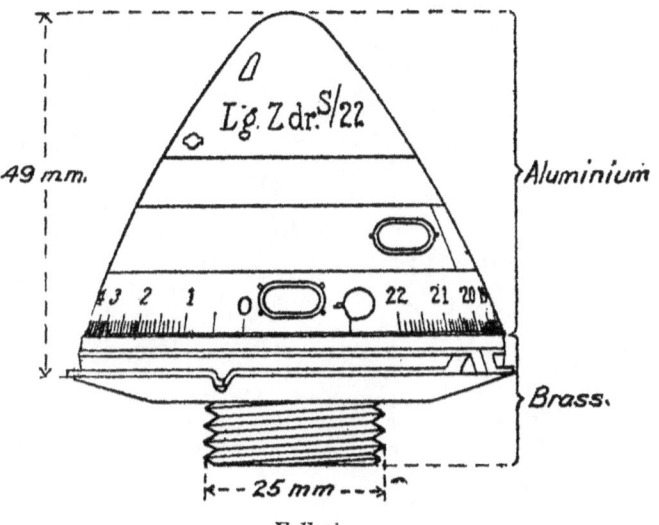

Full size.

111

Designation.—*Dopp. Z. 92 = Doppel-Zünder, 1892* (1892 pattern time and percussion fuze).

Used with.—

Gun.	Pattern of Shell.	Maximum range.	
		Time.	Perc'n.
		yards.	yards.
21 cm. howitzer in turret ..	'89 shrapnel (Ec.)	5,960	5,960
21 cm. gun with chase rings	'04 shrapnel	7,655	7,655
15 cm. howitzer in turret	'88, '14 and '14A H.E.	7,218	7,874
(15 cm.) heavy field howitzer	'88 H.E.	6,616	6,616
(15 cm.) heavy field howitzers, '02 and '13	Ditto	8,147	8,147
15 cm. long gun with chase rings	'15 shrapnel with forward driving band	7,929	7,929
15 cm. long gun with chase rings	'80/'92 shrapnel	7,655	7,655
15 cm. gun with chase rings	'80/'92 shrapnel, '15 shrapnel with forward driving band	7,546	7,546
15 cm. long gun	'90 or '90/'92, '07 and '15 shrapnel	8,968	10,936
12 cm. heavy gun {	'14 H.E.	—	7,983
	'80/'92, '15 shrapnel	7,218	7,983

Nature.—Time and percussion.

Graduations.—Graduated from $\frac{2}{8}$ to 28 in seconds and eighths of a second (lowest and highest figures are 1 and 28).

When the setting mark is opposite the cross, the fuze is set for percussion.

Material—Brass.

Remarks.—The fuze cap is painted red in fuzes of recent manufacture, which merely indicates the provision of a device for clamping the lower time ring on the shock of discharge.

The modern variation of this fuze is marked **Dopp. Z. 92 lg. Brlg.** or long-burning Dopp. Z. 92, the period of burning having been increased from 28 to 41 seconds. For description *see* page 118.

Dopp. Z. 92.

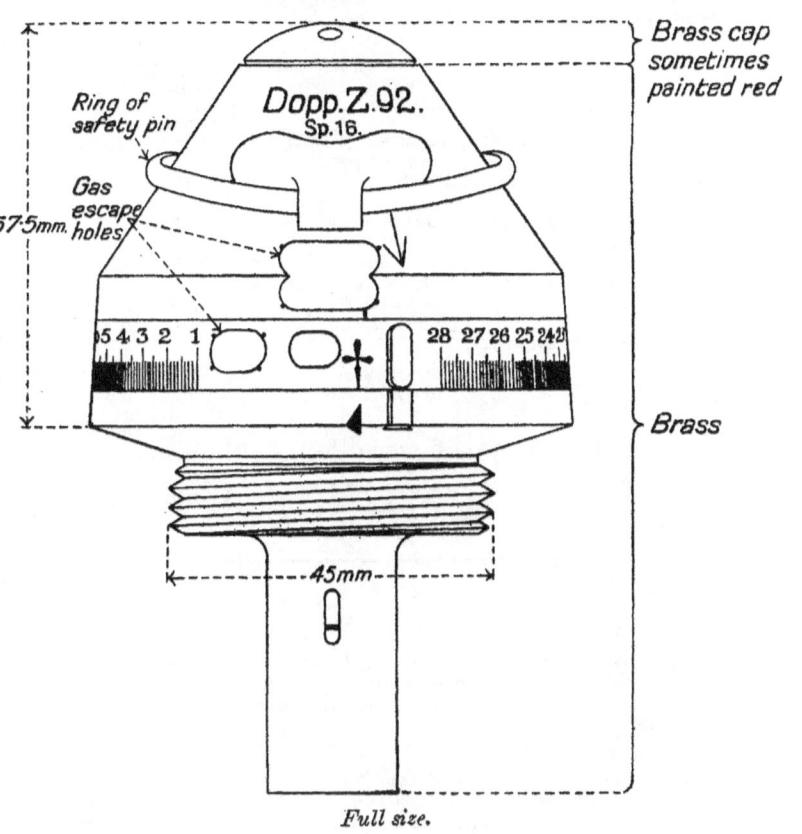

Full size.

Designation.—*Dopp. Z. 92 f. 10 cm. K.* = *Doppel-Zünder, 189 , für 10 cm. Kanone* (1892 pattern time and percussion fuze for 10 cm. gun).

Used with.—

(Dopp. Z. 92 K. 15 is also used with the shells given in the table except those marked with an asterisk.)

Gun.	Pattern of Shell.	Maximum range.	
		Time.	Perc'n.
		yards.	yards.
15 cm. gun on coast defence mounting '07	'03 shrapnel (gr.) and '03 shrapnel	8,530	8,530
15 cm. gun with overhead shield	Ditto	10,718	17,060
15 cm. experimental gun on wheeled carriage	'03 shrapnel (gr.) ...	12,249	18,592
13 cm. gun	13 cm. shrapnel ...	10,936	15,311
120 mm. French long gun	German-made shrapnel	...	...
10 cm. short gun in turret	{ 10 cm. H.E.	8,530	10.608
	'96 shrapnel	8,640	10,608
10 cm. gun with overhead shield			
10 cm. gun in turret ...	'96 shrapnel	9,296	11,811
10 cm. reinforced gun in turret	10 cm. H.E.*	9,186	11,811
10 cm. gun and 10 cm. gun '04	{ 10 cm. H.E.*	} 9,077	11,264
	'96 shrapnel		
10 cm. gun '14 and 10 cm. gun '97	{ 10 cm. H.E.*	} 9,296	12,085
	'96 shrapnel		
9 cm. gun	'15 shrapnel	6,124	7,109

Nature.—Time and percussion.

Graduations.—Graduated from $\frac{3}{8}$ to 26 in seconds and eighths of a second (lowest and highest figures are 1 and 26).

When the setting mark is opposite the cross, the fuze is set for percussion.

Material.—Brass.

Remarks.—A variation of this fuze has been found in which "*f. 10 cm. K.*" has been crossed out and "*lg. Brlg.*" has been substituted. It is graduated in seconds and quarters of a second from 2 to 41 (lowest and highest figures are 2 and 40).

Another variation of this fuze is marked **Dopp. Z. 92 K. 15**. In external appearance, graduation and material, it is identical with Dopp. Z. 92 für 10 cm. K. and is the same fuze with a shorter designation.

Dopp. Z. 92 f. 10 cm. K.

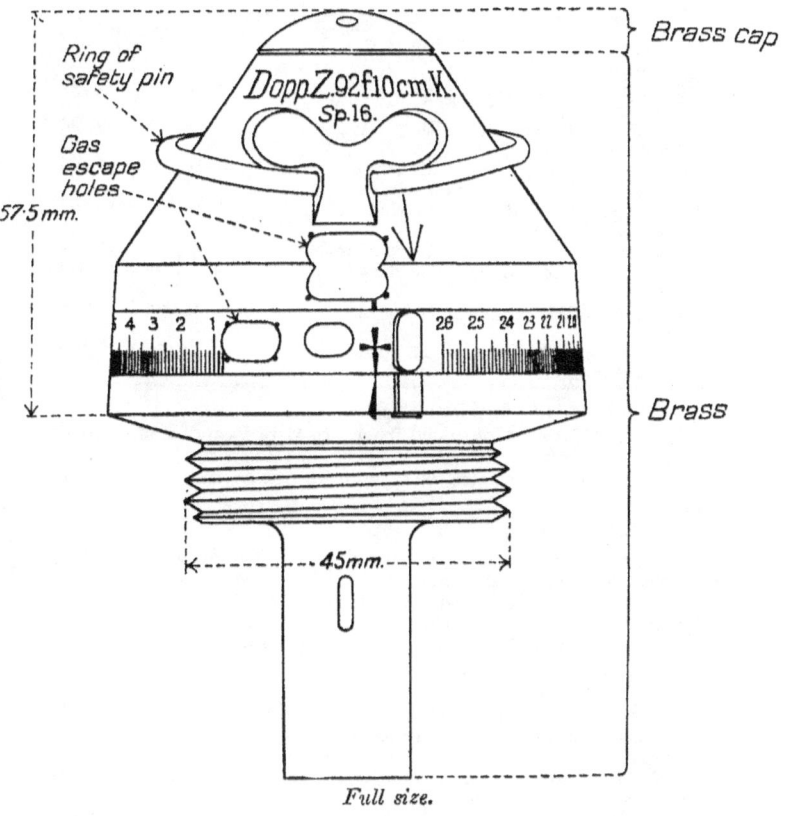

Full size.

Designation.—*Dopp. Z. 92 lg. Brlg.* = *Doppel-Zünder, 1892, lange Brennlänge* (1892 pattern long-burning time and percussion fuze).

Used with.—

Gun.	Shell.	Maximum range.	
		Time.	Perc'n.
		yards.	yards.
(15 cm.) heavy field howitzer	'14 H.E.	6,452	6,616
(15 cm.) heavy field howitzer '02	Ditto	8,147	8,147
(15 cm.) heavy field howitzer '13	Ditto	9,296	9,296
15 cm. gun with overhead shield	'03 shrapnel and '03 shrapnel (gr.)	16,186	17,060
15 cm. experimental gun on wheeled carriage	'03 shrapnel (gr.)	16,404	18,592
13 cm. gun	13 cm. shrapnel	15,311	15,311
10 cm. gun '04, 10 cm. gun	'96 shrapnel	11,264	11,264
10 cm. gun '14, 10 cm. gun '97	Ditto	12,085	12,085
9 cm. gun and 9 cm. anti-aircraft gun	'15 shrapnel	7,109	7,109

Nature.—Time and percussion.

Graduations.—Graduated from 2 to 41 in seconds and quarters of a second (lowest and highest figures are 2 and 40).

When the setting mark is opposite the cross, the fuze is set for percussion.

Material.—Brass.

Remarks.—This long-burning fuze was introduced in order to increase the range with time fuze of the more modern howitzers and high velocity guns with which Dopp. Z. 92 and Dopp. Z. 92 f. 10 cm. K. were formerly used.

When it was first introduced, a few specimens were found marked Dopp. Z. 92 $\frac{\text{f. 10 cm. K.}}{\text{lg. Brlg.}}$

A green cap is said to denote a fuze graduated up to 42 seconds, but specimens with a green cap have been found graduated up to 41 only.

For variations of this fuze marked **Dopp. Z. 92 lg. Brlg. n.F.** and **Dopp. Z. 92 n.F.**, *see* page 120.

Another variation of this fuze is marked **Dopp. Z. 92 lg. Brlg. o.Az** The letters "o.Az." are painted on in red. This fuze has no percussion system. It is used for anti-aircraft work with the 1914 pattern 9 cm. H.E. shell (grey) and with the 1915 pattern 9 cm. shrapnel (blue), fired by the '73 pattern 9 cm. anti-aircraft gun.

Dopp. Z. 92 lg. Brlg.

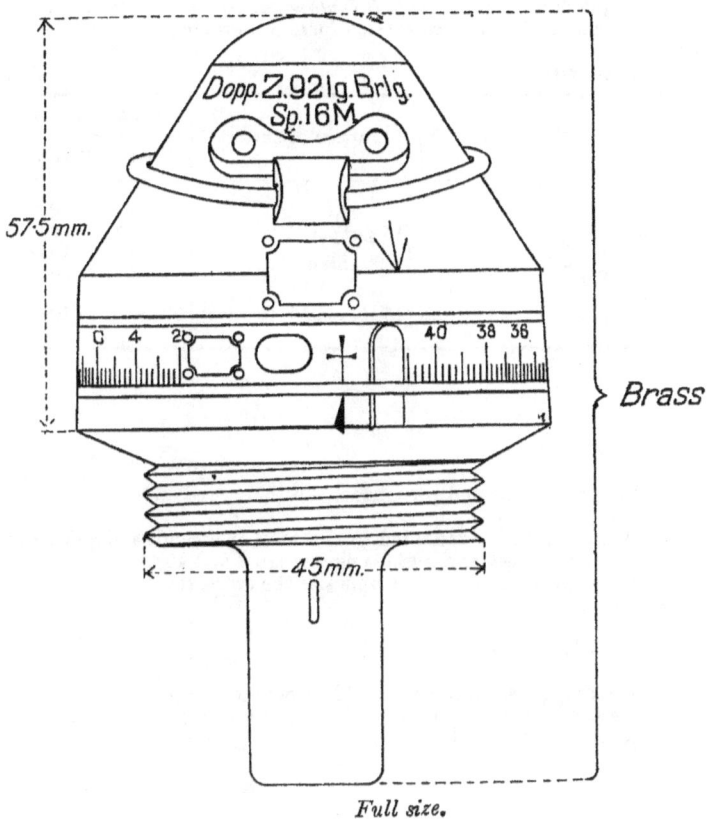

Full size.

Designation.—*Dopp. Z. 92 lg. Brlg. n.F.* or *Dopp. Z. 92 n.F. = Doppel-Zünder, 1892, lange Brennlänge neuer Form* (1892 pattern long-burning time and percussion fuze, of new shape).

Used with.—

Gun.	Pattern of Shell.	Maximum range.	
		Time.	Perc'n.
		yards.	yards.
15 cm. long gun	'15 shrapnel	10,936 ?	10,936 ?
10 cm. gun '04, 10 cm. gun '14, 10 cm. gun '97	} '96 shrapnel ...	{ 11,264 ? 12,085 ?	11,264 ? 12,085 ?
9 cm. gun	'15 shrapnel	7,109 ?	7,109 ?

Nature.—Time and percussion.

Graduations.—Graduated from 2 to 41 in seconds and quarters of a second (lowest and highest figures are 2 and 40).

When the setting mark is opposite the cross, the fuze is set for percussion.

Material.—Brass.

Remarks.—A green cap is said to denote a fuze graduated up to 42 seconds, but specimens with a green cap have been found graduated up to 41 only.

Dopp. Z. 92 lg. Brlg. n.F.
or
Dopp. Z. 92 n.F.

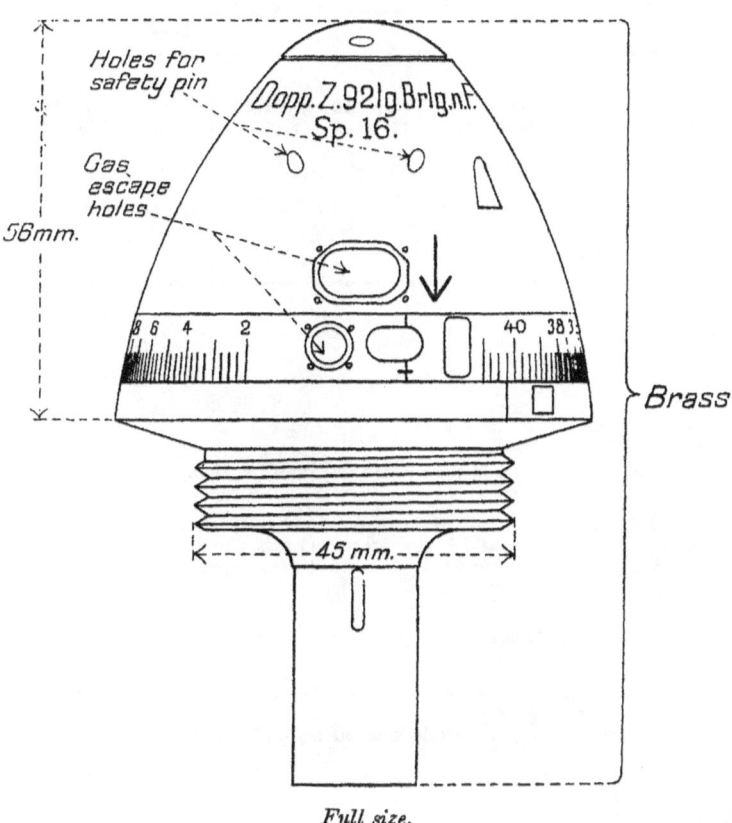

Full size.

Designation.—*Dopp. Z. 15 = Doppel-Zünder, 1915* (1915 pattern time and percussion fuze).

Used with.—

Gun.	Pattern of Shell.	Maximum range.	
		Time.	Perc'n.
		yards.	yards.
(15 cm.) heavy field howitzer	'12 and '12 n/A. H.E....	6,616 ?	6,616 ?
(15 cm.) heavy field howitzer '02	Ditto	8,147 ?	8,147 ?
(15 cm.) heavy field howitzer '13	Ditto	8,968	8,968 ?
(15 cm.) long heavy field howitzer '13	Ditto	9,296 ?	9,296 ?
15 cm. long gun	Ditto	10,936 ?	10,936 ?

Nature.—Time and percussion (with and without delay action).

Graduations.—Graduated from 2 to 41 in seconds and quarters of a second (lowest and highest figures are 2 and 40).

When the setting mark is opposite the cross, the fuze is set for percussion.

Material.—Brass and steel.

Remarks.—The same gaine is used with this fuze as with Gr. Z. 04 (*see* page 68).

A variation of this fuze is marked **Dopp. Z. 15 umg.**

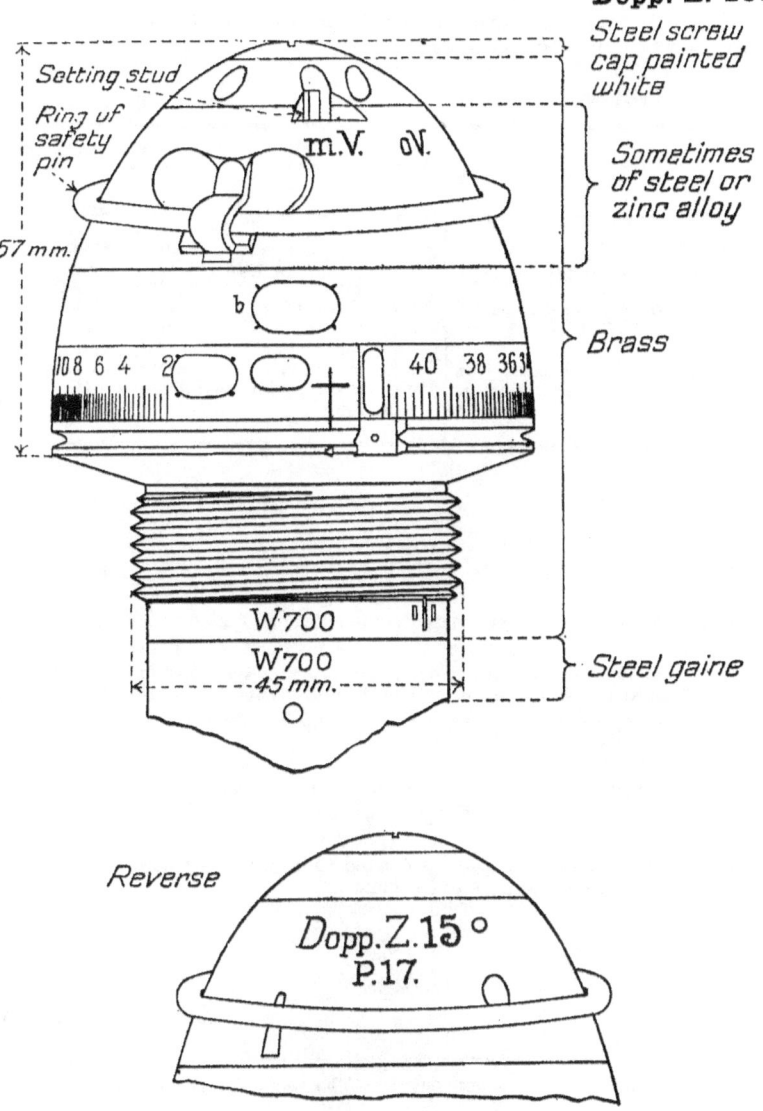

Dopp. Z. 15.

Designation.—*Dopp. Z. 16 = Doppel-Zünder, 1916* (1916 pattern time and percussion fuze).

Used with.—

Gun.	Pattern of Shell.	Maximum range.	
		Time.	Perc'n.
24 cm. naval gun ...	24 cm. shrapnel with false cap	yards. at least 22,000	yards. at least 22,000
15 cm. gun with overhead shield (K.i.S.L.)	'03 (gr.)* shrapnel ... '03 (gr.)* shrapnel with false cap	17,060 over 17,060	17,060 over 17,060
15 cm. experimental gun on wheeled carriage (K.i.R.L.)	'03 (gr.)* shrapnel ... '03 (gr.)* shrapnel with false cap	18,592 over 18,592	18,592 over 18,592

Nature.—Time and percussion clockwork fuze.

Graduations.—Nil. To set the fuze, the steel housing is turned by means of a fuze setter to the desired position. A stud on the housing, and a stud and a recess on the base serve as the points of application of the fuze setter.

Material.—Brass body, with steel cap and steel housing; aluminium housing for the percussion system.

Remarks.—This fuze is reported to be extremely accurate. It is chiefly used against kite balloons.

---

* (gr.) probably = *grau* or grey. This shrapnel is painted grey.

Dopp. Z. 16.

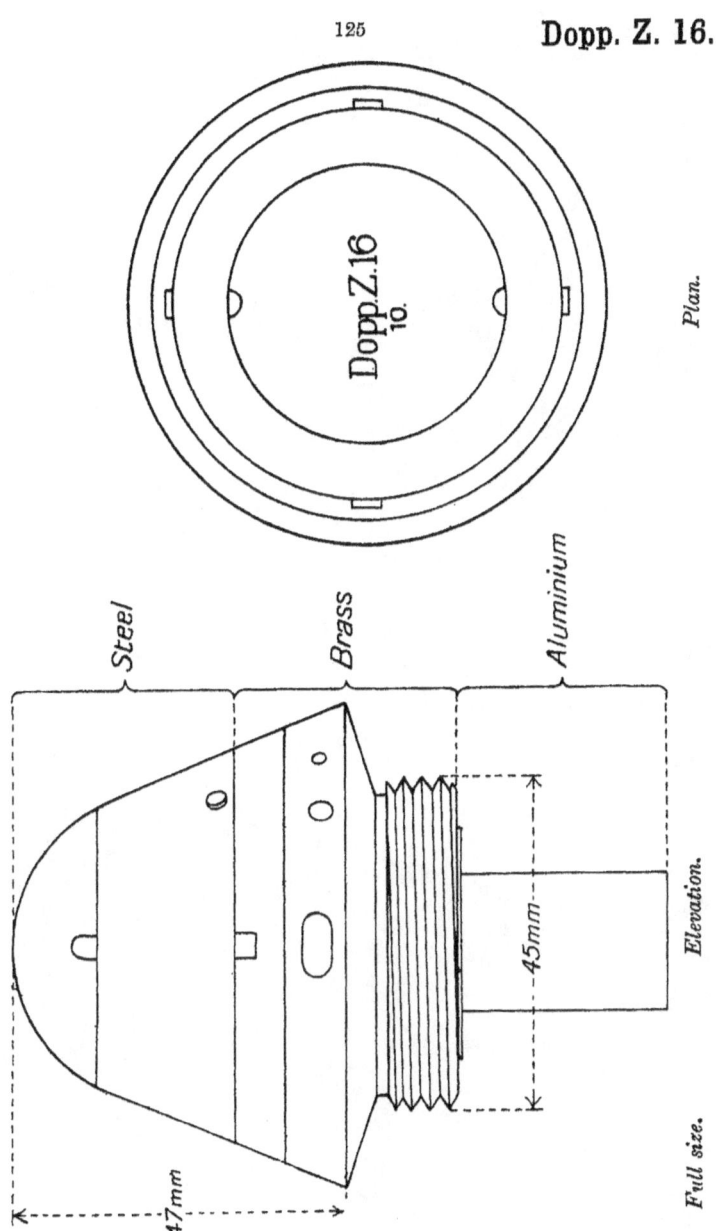

Plan.

Elevation.

Full size.

129

FUZES FOR UNIVERSAL SHELL.

Designation.—*K.Z.11 l.B.* = *Kanonen-Zünder, 1911, lange Brennlänge* (1911 pattern long-burning gun fuze).

Used with.—

Gun.	Pattern of Shell.	Maximum range.	
		Time.	Perc'n.
(7·7 cm.) field gun (96 n/A.)	Universal shell...	yards. 7,874	yards. 9,186

Nature.—Triple action (with universal shell)—
1. Time : shrapnel bursts in air, H.E. head flies on and detonates.
2. Time : whole shell detonates in air.
3. Percussion.

Graduations.—Graduated from 2 to 72 in hundreds of metres (50 = 5,000 metres); each of the smallest divisions from 2 to 15 is equivalent to 100 metres of range, those from 15 to 72 are equivalent to 50 metres.

G = Granate or H.E. effect ; **S = Schrapnel** or Shrapnel.

As shown in the plate, the fuze is set for percussion shrapnel.

The original pattern **K. Z. 11** fuze was graduated from 2 to 50 in hundreds of metres, and a later pattern was graduated up to 70 (the maximum ranges with time fuzes being 5,468 and 7,655 yards, respectively). There was also a corrector scale on the lower time ring to raise or lower the height of burst.

Material.—Aluminium body, steel cap. The gaine is sometimes made of aluminium and grooved longitudinally.

Remarks.—This fuze was largely used by 7·7 cm. anti-aircraft guns with universal shell.

An official document issued by the War Ministry stated that universal shell, and consequently this fuze, would become obsolete from the 1st July, 1916 ; both are, however, sometimes met with.

K.Z.11 1.B.

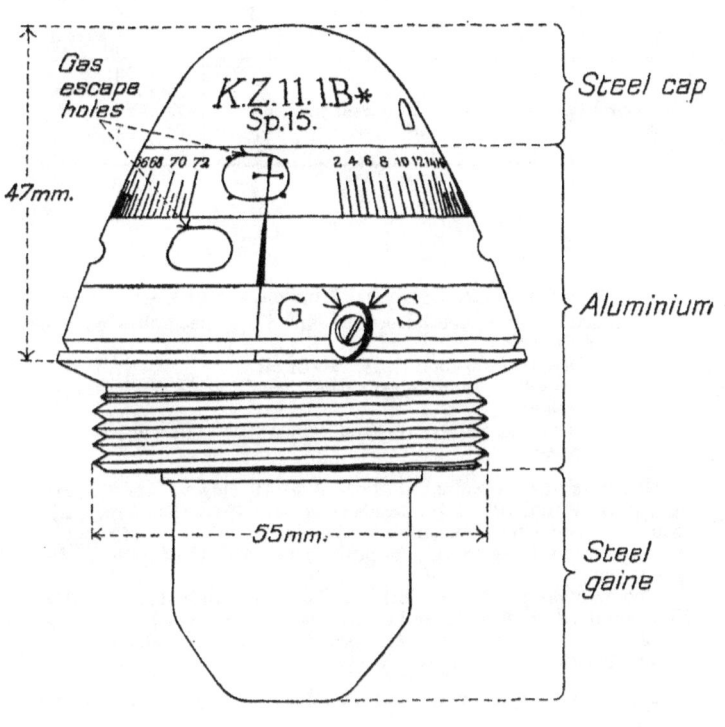

Full size.

Designation.—*H.Z. 05 l.B. = Haubitz - Zünder, 1905, lange Brennlänge* (1905 pattern long-burning howitzer fuze).

Used with.—

Gun.	Pattern of Shell.	Maximum range.	
		Time.	Perc'n.
(10·5 cm.) light field howitzer '98/'09	Universal shell...	yards. 7,655	yards. 7,655

Nature.— Quadruple action (with universal shell)—
1. Time : shrapnel bursts in air, H.E. head flies on and detonates.
2. Time : whole shell detonates in air.
3. Percussion : non-delay action, whole shell detonates on impact.
4. Percussion : delay action, whole shell detonates after impact.

Graduations.—Graduated from 3 to 70 (lowest and highest figures are 3 and 70) in hundreds of metres (52 = 5,200 metres); each of the smallest divisions is equivalent to 50 metres of range.

When the setting mark is opposite the cross, the fuze is set for percussion.

The original pattern of **H.Z. 05** fuze was graduated from 3 to 53 in hundreds of metres, and a later pattern was graduated up to 63, the maximum ranges with time fuze being 5,796 and 6,890 yards, respectively.

Material.—Brass, with two aluminium rings, steel cap and steel gaine.

Remarks.—An official document issued by the War Ministry stated that universal shell, and consequently this fuze, would become obsolete on the 1st July, 1916 ; both are, however, sometimes met with.

H.Z.05 1.B.

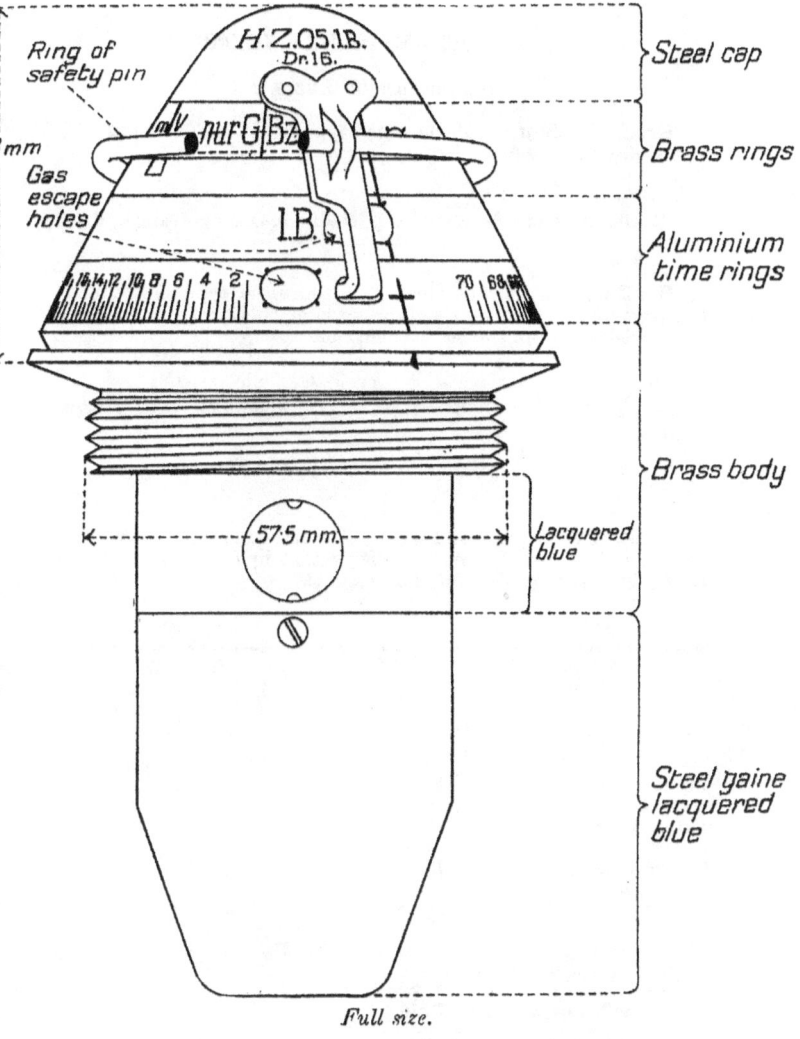

Full size.

OBSOLETE ARTILLERY FUZES.

(a) Percussion Fuzes.

Gr. Z. 84.—Brass. Of the same type as *Gr. Z. 82* (*see* page 65). Non-delay action only.

Used with.—

21 cm. Mortar: 1888 pattern shell: maximum range, 9,952 yards.

Gr. Z. 96.—Brass and steel. Of the same type as *Gr. Z. 04* (*see* page 69). There were two patterns of this fuze, one could be set for delay action, the other could not.

Used with.—

21 cm. Mortar: 1883 pattern shell: maximum range, 9,733 yards.

21 cm. Mortar: 1896 pattern shell: maximum range, 10,280 yards.

Gr. Z. 96/04.—Brass and steel. Of the same type as *Gr. Z. 04* (*see* page 69). Can be set for delay action by means of a setting stud. This fuze is illustrated on page 137.

Used with.—

Gun.	Pattern of Shell.	Maximum range, percussion.
		yards.
21 cm. mortar	'88 H.E.	8,968
"Mortar" (21 cm.)	Ditto	9,952
(15 cm.) heavy field howitzer	'83, '96, '04, '14 and '14A H.E.	6,616
(15 cm.) heavy field howitzer '02	Ditto	8,147
(15 cm.) heavy field howitzer '13	Ditto	9,296
15 cm. long gun	'14 and '14A H.E.	10,936
15 cm. long gun with chase rings	'14 and '14A H.E., with forward driving band	8,749
15 cm. gun with chase rings	Ditto	8,640

Gr. Z. 96/04.
Bd. Z. 06.

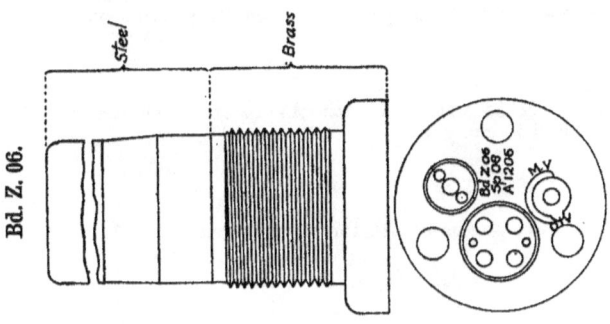

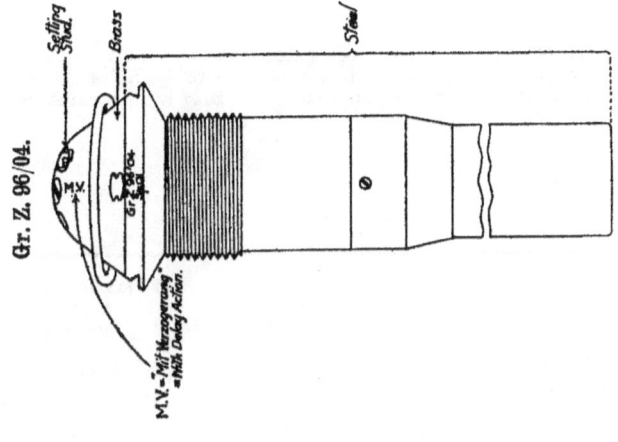

Half scale.

Kz. Gr. Z. 14 and **G. Gr. Z. 14.**—Brass with steel cap. Of the same type as *Gr. Z. 14* (*see* page 71). Non-delay action only.

Kz. Gr. Z. 14 was used with the 15 cm. long gun, 15 cm. howitzer and 13 cm. gun.

G. Gr. Z. 14 was used with the 15 cm. howitzer.

15 cm. Gr. C/14.—This was really a steel fuze-hole socket to take a percussion fuze of the same type as *Gr. Z. 82* and fitted with a steel cap similar to the one shown on page 65. Non-delay action only. Used with a 15 cm. gun of older pattern.

Bd. Z. 06.—Brass with steel gaine. A base fuze, with or without delay action, similar in appearance to *lg. Bd. Z. 10* (*see* page 83), by which it was superseded. This fuze is illustrated on page 137.

Used with.—

Gun.	Pattern of Shell.	Maximum range, percussion.
		yards.
23 cm. howitzer	'06 H.E.	12,030
21 cm. mortar	'96 H.E.	10,280
21 cm. mortar (bronze)	'06 H.E.	8,530
15 cm. coast defence gun	Ditto	8,530
13 cm. gun	H.E. shell	15,748

(b) Time and Percussion Fuzes.

Dopp. Z. 86.—Brass with steel cap. Graduated from 1 to 13 in seconds and also from 3 to 31 in hundreds of metres. This fuze is illustrated on page 141.

Used with.—

9 cm. field gun '73/'88 : 1882 pattern shrapnel : maximum range (time fuze), 3,390 yards.

Dopp. Z. 88.—Time and percussion fuze. Resembled *Dopp. Z. 86* (*see* page 141).

Used with.—

12 cm. gun : 1888 a/A. pattern shell : maximum range (percussion), 7,984 yards.

Dopp. Z. 91.—Brass. Graduated from 3 to 45 in hundreds of metres. This fuze is illustrated on page 141.

Used with.—

9 cm. field gun '73/'88 : 1888 pattern shell and 1891 pattern shrapnel : maximum range (time fuze), 4,921 yards.

Dopp. Z. 92 f. FH.—Brass. Graduated from 5 to 56 in hundreds of metres. This fuze is similar in appearance to *Dopp. Z. 92* (*see* page 115).

Used with. —

(10·5 cm.) light field howitzer '98/'09 : 1898 pattern shell : maximum range (time fuze), 6,124 yards.

Dopp. Z. 96.—Brass and aluminium with steel cap. Graduated from 4 to 50 in hundreds of metres. This fuze is similar in appearance to *Dopp. Z. 96 n/A.* (*see* page 91), by which it was superseded.

Used with.—

(7·7 cm.) field gun (96 n/A.) and 7·7 cm. gun on casemate mounting : '96 H.E. and shrapnel : maximum range (time fuze), 5,468 yards.

Dopp. Z. 98.—Brass. Graduated from 3 to 56 in hundreds of metres. This fuze is illustrated on page 141.

Used with.—

(10·5 cm.) light field howitzer '98/'09 : 1898 pattern shrapnel : maximum range (time fuze), 6,120 yards.

Dopp. Z. 08.—A clockwork fuze. The housing is of aluminium. It did not prove a success and has only been found on flares dropped from aircraft. It was intended for use with shrapnel fired from high velocity guns. This fuze is illustrated on page 141.

(c) Fuzes for Universal Shell.

K.Z. 11.—*See* page 132.
H.Z. 05.—*See* page 135.

Dopp. Z. 86.
Dopp. Z. 91.
Dopp. Z. 98.
Dopp. Z. 08.

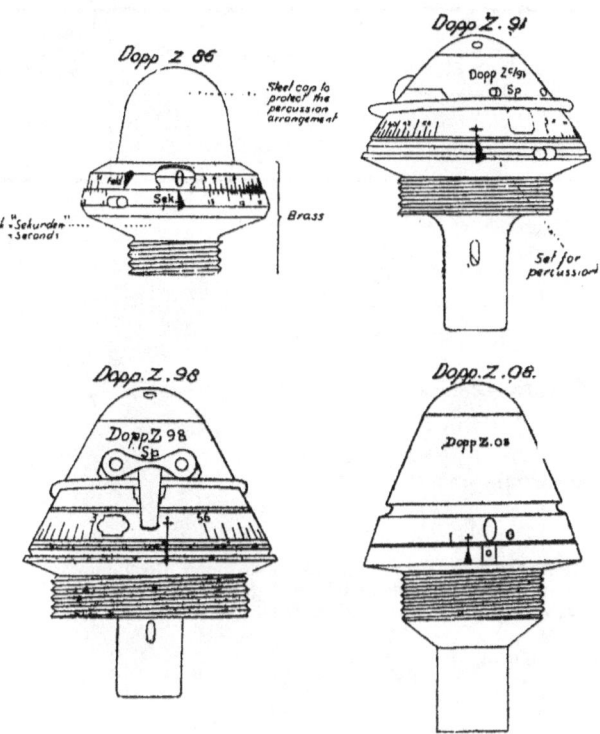

Approx. half full size.

NAVAL FUZES.

(a) Percussion Fuzes.

Designation.—*Z. f. 3·7 cm. Spgr.* = *Zünder für 3·7 cm. Sprenggranate* (fuze for **3·7** cm. H.E. shell).

Used with.—

Gun.	Pattern of Shell.	Maximum range, percussion.
3·7 cm. trench gun...	3·7 cm. H.E.	yards. —

Nature.—Percussion.

Material.—

Remarks.—It is stated in a German document that the maximum effective range of this gun against shields, loophole plates, sandbag revetments, &c., is 656 yards.

Z. f. 3·7 cm. Spgr.

Designation.—*Granat-Zünder C/98* (1898 pattern fuze for H.E. shell). *C= Construction* (i.e., *pattern*).

Used with.—

Gun.	Pattern of Shell.	Maximum range, percussion.
8·8 cm. Q.F. gun L/30	H.E. Shell L/2·6	yards. 9,077
8·8 cm. Q.F. gun L/35	Ditto	over 9,000
8·8 cm. Q.F. gun L/45	H.E. Shell L/3·6	over 9,000

Nature.—Percussion.

Material.—Brass.

Remarks.—

Granat-Zünder C/98.

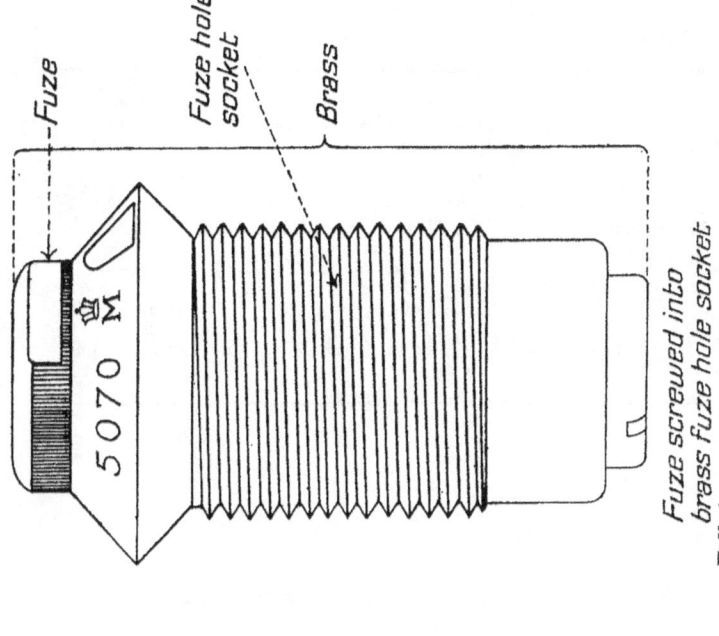

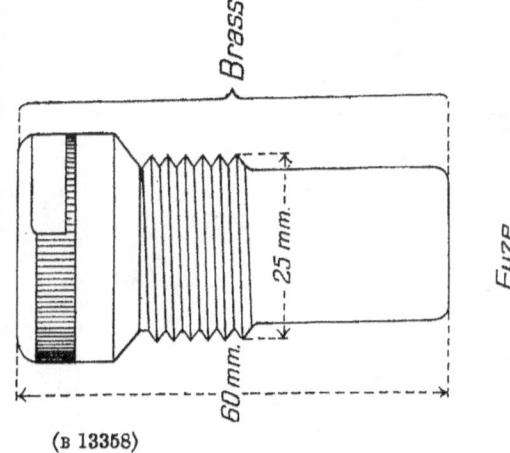

Designation.—Percussion fuze for naval shell.

Used with.—

Gun.	Pattern of Shell.	Maximum range, percussion.
		yards.
15 cm. gun L/30 ...	*15 cm. Spgr. L/3·6* ...	13,233
15 cm. Q.F. gun L/40	*15 cm. Spgr. L/5 (Dz.) (Haube.)*	20,451
	15 cm. Spgr. L/3·6 ...	About 14,983
10·5 cm. Q.F. gun L/35 ...	*10·5 cm. Spgr. L/3·6 (Kz.)*	About 10,389

Nature.—Percussion nose fuze, with centrifugal safety device.

Material.—Steel, with brass cap, and brass gaine containing the exploder in a tinned brass case.

Remarks.—Used in conjunction with a delay action exploder *Gr. Zdlg. C/98 m. 0·05 Sek. Verz.* (*Grosse Zündladung Construction 1898 mit 0·05 Sekunden Verzögerung* = large 1898 pattern exploder ; delay, 0·05 second).

Some specimens of this fuze are made in one piece without a cap.

Percussion Fuze for Naval Shell.

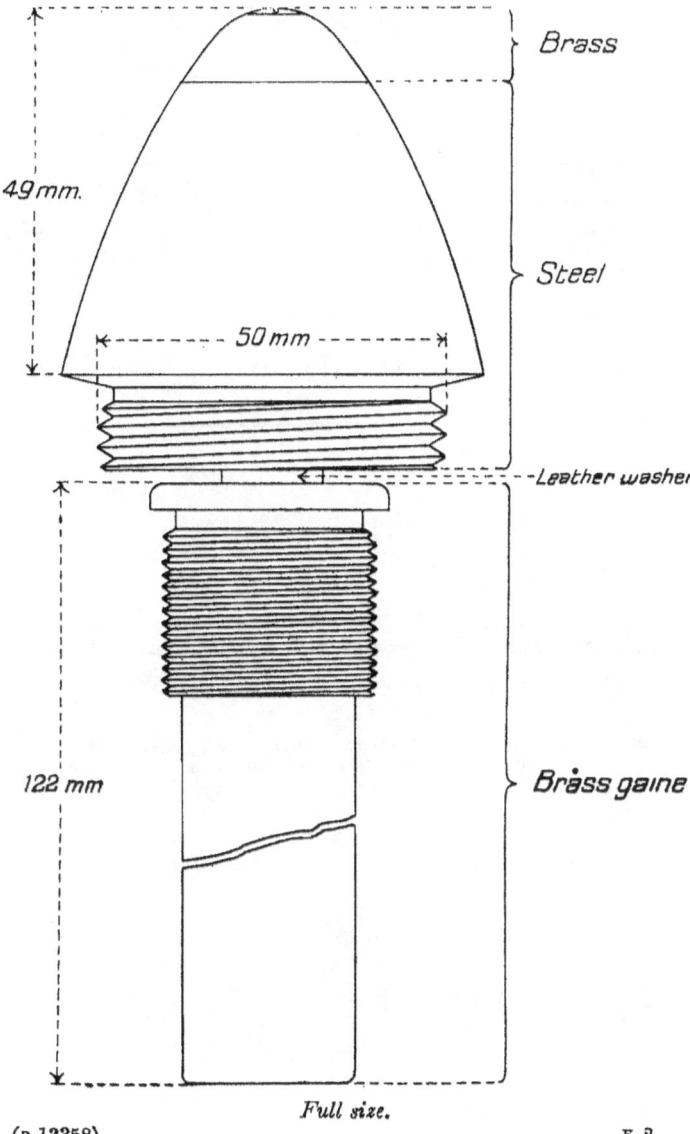

Full size.

Designation.—Percussion fuze for 17 cm. shell.

Used with.—

Gun.	Pattern of Shell.	Maximum range, percussion.
17 cm. Q.F. gun L/40 ...	*17 cm. Spgr. L/3 (Kz.)*...	yards. Over 16,000

Nature.—Percussion nose fuze with centrifugal safety device.

Material.—Brass, with brass gaine containing the exploder in a tinned brass case.

Remarks.—Used in conjunction with a delay action exploder *Zalg. C/98 m. 0·05 Sek. Verz.* (*Zündladung Construction 1898 mit 0·05 Sekunden Verzögerung* = 1898 pattern exploder; delay 0·05 second.)

Percussion Fuze for 17 cm. Shell.

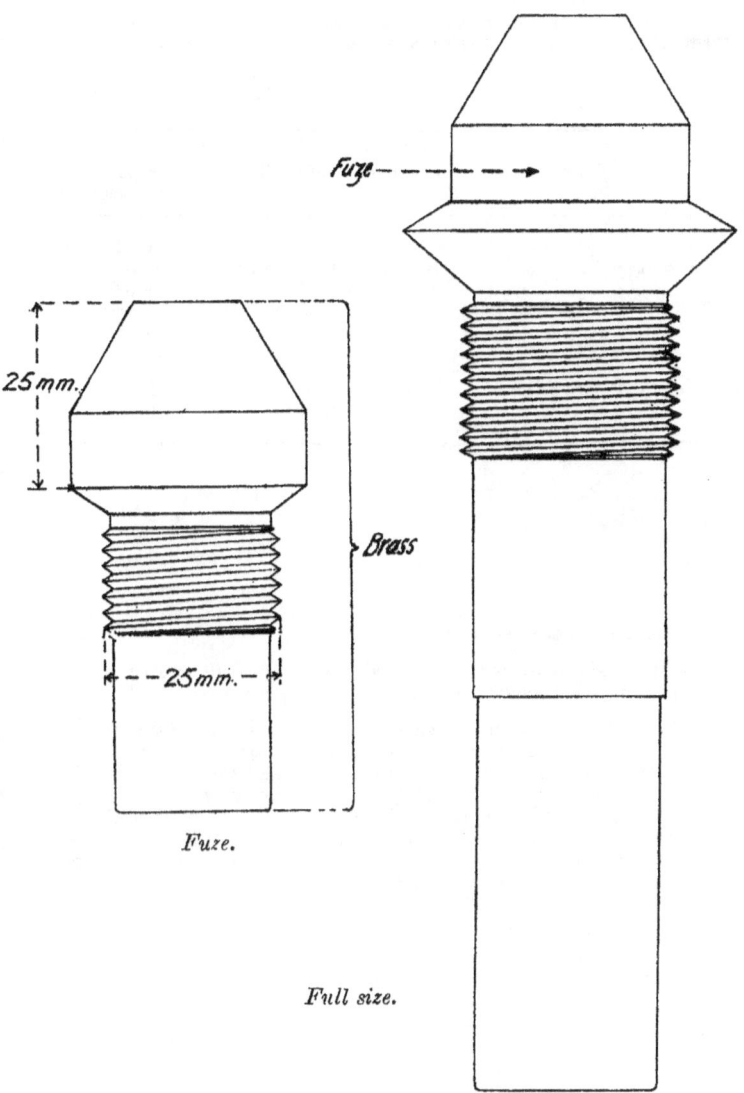

Fuze.

Full size.

Fuze, screwed into brass gaine.

Designation.—*Spgr. m.K.* = *Sprenggranatenzünder mit Klappensicherung* (fuze with centrifugal safety device for H.E. shell).

Used with.—

Gun.	Pattern of Shell.	Maximum range, percussion.
		yards.
38 cm. gun	H.E. shell with false cap } Tapered H.E. shell	at least 46,000
35·6 cm. coast defence gun	H.E. shell with false cap	at least 50,300
24 cm. Q.F. gun	Ditto	29,090
21 cm. Q.F. gun L/45 ...	Ditto ... ... Tapered H.E. shell ...	29,200 29,200 ?

Nature.—Percussion fuze.

Material.—Lacquered steel body, with brass cap; steel gaine containing the exploder in a tinned brass case.

Remarks.—A copper gas-check fits over the base of the fuze.

With this fuze is used a delay action exploder (delay 0·05 second). Two sizes are made, one "long" and the other "short," known as *lg. Zdlg. C/08* and *Zdlg. C/08*, respectively.

A variation of this fuze, *with delay action*, is used with the 38 cm. naval H.E. shell. It is marked **m.V.u.K.** (*mit Verzögerung und Klappensicherung* = with delay action and centrifugal safety device) and not Spgr. m.K.

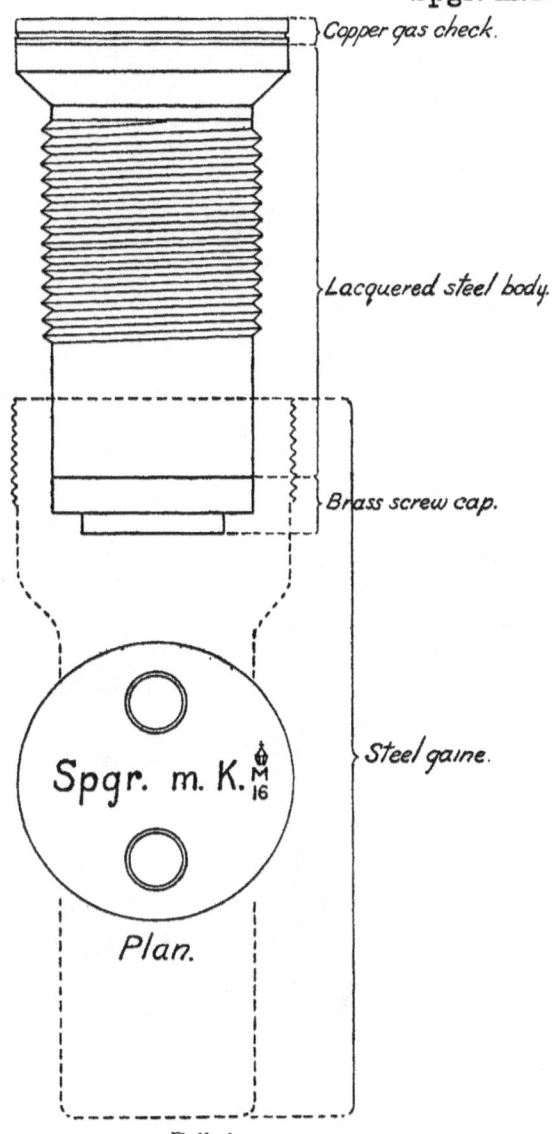

153

(b) Time and Percussion Fuzes.*

Designation.—*Dopp. Z. S/26 = Doppel-Zünder, 26 Sekunden* (time and percussion fuze, 26 seconds).

Used with.—

Gun.	Pattern of Shell.	Maximum range.	
		Time.	Perc'n.
8·8 cm. Q.F. gun ...	8·8 cm. *Spgr.* L/3·7 (*Dz.*)	yards.	yards.

Nature.—Time and percussion.

Graduations.—Graduated from 1 to 26 in seconds and fifths of a second (lowest and highest figures are 1 and 26).

When the setting mark is opposite the cross, the fuze is set for percussion.

Material.—Brass body with cap of zinc alloy.

Remarks.—

---

* For the clockwork time fuze, **Dopp. Z. 16**, *see* page 124.

Dopp. Z. S/26.

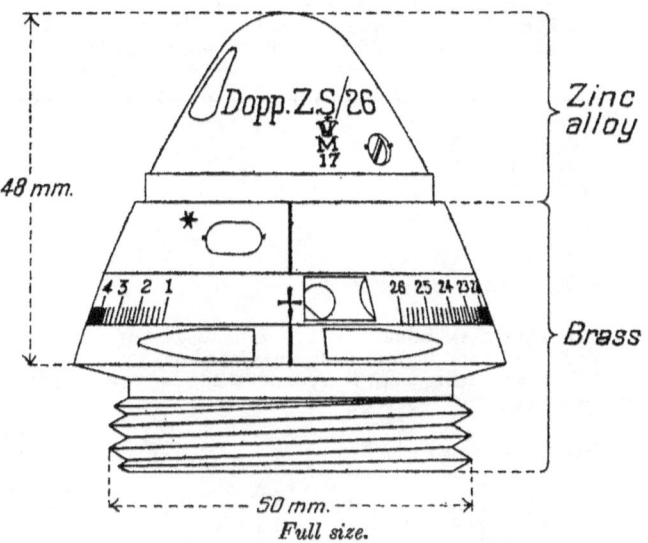

Full size.

Designation.—*Dopp. Z. S/43 = Doppel-Zünder, 43 Sekunden* (time and percussion fuze, 43 seconds).

Used with.—

Gun.	Pattern of Shell.	Maximum range.	
		Time.	Perc'n.
15 cm. gun L/30	*15 cm. Spgr. L/3·6*	yards. ?	yards. ?
15 cm. Q.F. gun L/40	*15 cm. Spgr. L/3·6 (Dz.)*	14,983	14,983
10·5 cm. Q.F. gun L/35	*10·5 cm. Spgr. L/3·6 (Kz.)*	10,389	10,389

Nature.—Time and percussion.

Graduations.—Graduated from 1 to 43 in seconds and fifths of a second (lowest and highest figures are 1 and 43).
When the setting mark is opposite the cross, the fuze is set for percussion.

Material.—Brass.

Remarks.—Used in conjunction with a delay action exploder *Zdlg. C/98 m. 0·05 Sek. Verz.* (*Zündladung Construction 1898 mit 0·05 Sekunden Verzögerung* = 1898 pattern exploder; delay 0·05 second.)

Dopp. Z. S/43.

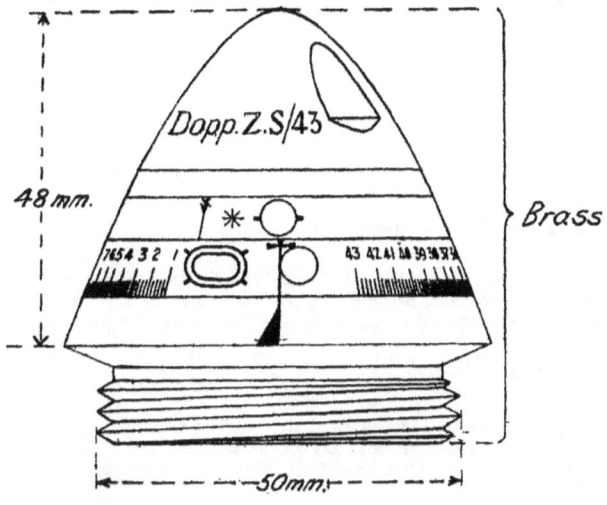

Full size.

Designation.—*Dopp. Z. S./56* (?) = *Doppel-Zünder, 56 Sekunden* (time and percussion fuze, 56 seconds).

Used with.—

Gun.	Pattern of Shell.	Maximum range, percussion.
15 cm. Q.F. Gun L/40 ?	*15 cm. Spgr. L/3˙6* (*Dz.*)	yards.

Nature.—Time and percussion.

Graduations.—Graduated from 1 to 56 in seconds and half seconds (lowest and highest figures are 1 and 56). When the setting mark is opposite the cross, the fuze is set for percussion.

Material.—Brass.

Remarks.—This fuze is probably used in conjunction with a delay action exploder marked *Zdlg.C/98 m. 0˙05 Sek. Verz.* (*Zündladung Construction 1898 mit 0˙05 Sekunden Verzögerung* = 1898 pattern exploder; delay, 0˙05 second.)

Dopp. Z. 56.

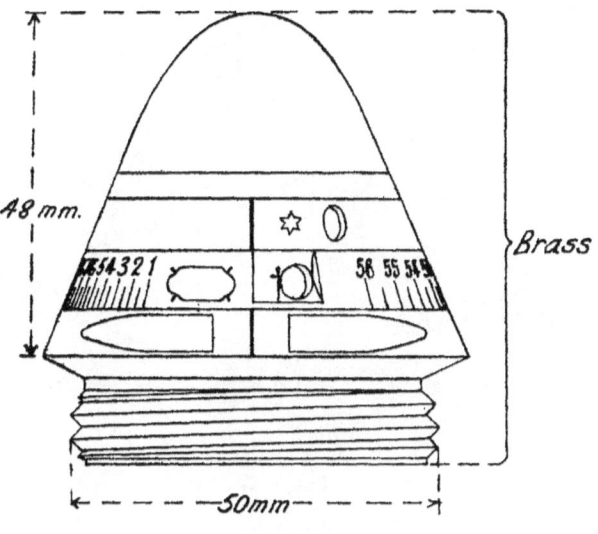

Full size.

169

"MINENWERFER" FUZES.

(a) Percussion Fuzes.

Designation.—*Az.16 f.l. W.M.* = *Aufschlag-Zünder, 1916, für leichte Wurf-Mine* (1916 pattern percussion fuze for light *Minenwerfer* shell).

Used with.—

Minenwerfer.	Pattern of Shell.	Maximum range, percussion.
7·6 cm. light *Minenwerfer* (original pattern)	'16 light H.E.	yards. 1,148
7·6 cm. new light *Minenwerfer*	Ditto	1,422

Nature.—Percussion.

Material.—

Remarks.—It is claimed that this new fuze will act on percussion, irrespective of the position in which the projectile strikes the ground.

Az. 16 f.l.W.M.

Designation.—

Used with.—

Gun.	Pattern of Shell.	Maximum range, percussion.
24 cm. heavy *Minenwerfer* (*Flügelminenwerfer*)	Heavy H.E. shell fitted with vanes	yards. 1,312

Nature.—Percussion : with or without delay action.
According to a German document, the non-delay fuze is practically instantaneous.

Material.—

Remarks.—According to a German document, the heavy H.E. shell fitted with the delay-action fuze has great penetrative effect. It will penetrate mined dug-outs with 23—30 feet of earth cover. Craters in average soil, 16—20 feet deep and 26—33 feet in diameter.

Two fuzes are issued with each bomb :—
    A non-delay action fuze, which is neither painted nor marked.
    A delay-action fuze, which is painted brown and marked *m. V.*

Percussion fuze for "Flügelminenwerfer" H.E. Shell.

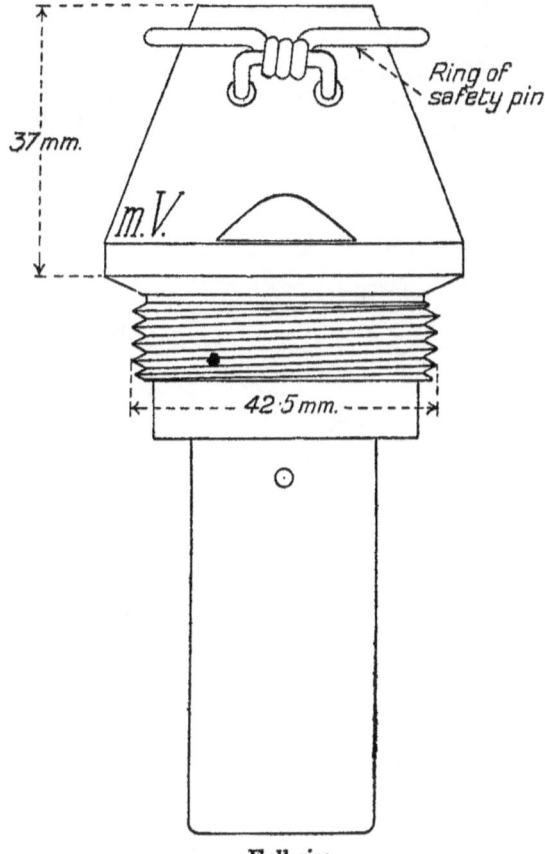

Full size.

The drawing shows a delay-action fuze. The non-delay fuze is identical externally, except for the painting and marking.

175

(b) Time and Percussion Fuzes.

Designation.—*l. W.M. Zdr. 2 = leichter Wurf-Mine-Zünder 2* (Mark 2 fuze for light *Minenwerfer* shell).

Used with.—

Minenwerfer.	Pattern of Shell.	Maximum range, time and percussion.
		yards.
7·6 cm. light *Minenwerfer* (original pattern)	Light H.E. (original pattern) '16 light H.E. ... Message shell (*l.N.M.*)... Light gas shell ...	1,148
7·6 cm. new light *Minenwerfer*	'16 light H.E. ... Message shell (*l.N.M.*)...	1,422
	Light gas shell ...	1,148

Nature.—Time and percussion.

Graduations.—Graduated from 7 to 24 in seconds and fifths of a second (lowest and highest figures are 7 and 24).

When the setting mark is opposite the cross, the fuze is set for percussion.

This fuze is an improved pattern of the original fuze, which was marked **l.W.M. Zdr.** and was graduated as above.

Material.—Brass, or brass with zinc cap.

Remarks.—The fuze is generally used as a percussion fuze, but is set to act by time from 1 to 4 seconds after impact, as a precaution in case the percussion arrangement misses fire.

The fuze cover used for night firing is shown in the plate. It is made of thin sheet iron, japanned black, and clips or screws on to the recess in the head of the fuze.

The original pattern of this fuze terminated in a powerful detonator; the exploder was placed in the top of the tin containing the bursting charge. The present pattern is screwed into the usual type of steel gaine containing the exploder.

l.W.M. Zdr. 2.

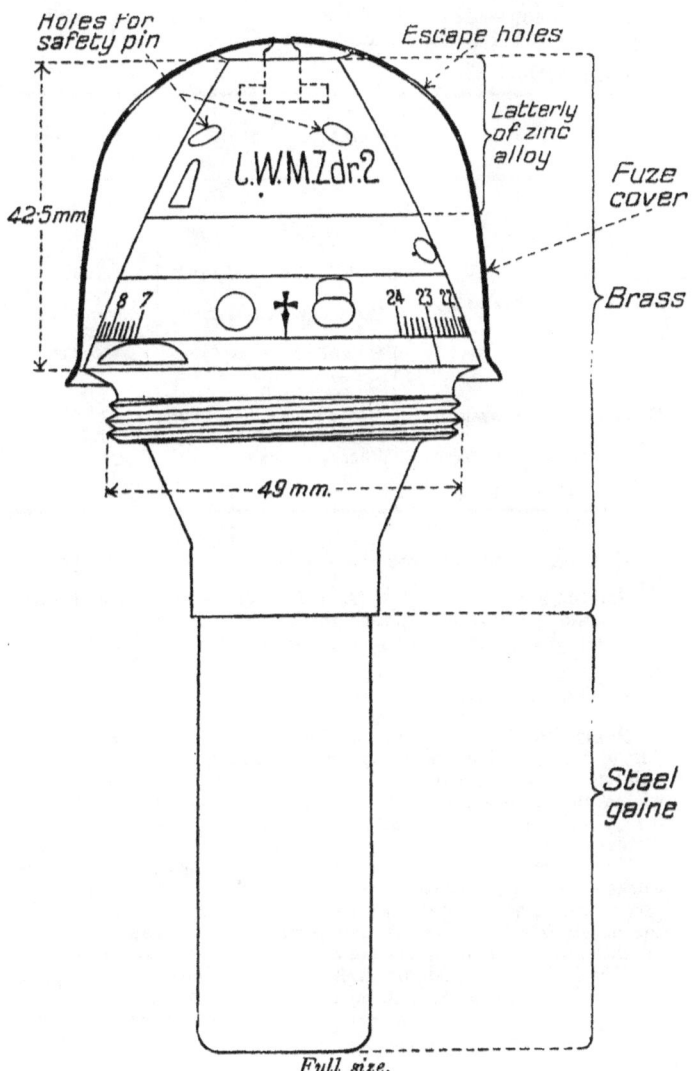

Full size.

Designation.—*Z.s.u.m. W.M.* = *Zünder schwerer und mittlerer Wurf-Mine* (fuze for heavy and medium *Minenwerfer* shell).

Used with.—

Minenwerfer.	Pattern of Shell.	Maximum range, time and percussion.
		yards.
	Full-sized heavy H.E.	514
	'16 half-sized heavy H.E.	930*
25 cm. heavy *Minenwerfer*	'16 quarter-sized heavy H.E.	over 1,200
	Half-sized heavy gas shell	930*
	'16 medium H.E.	1,000*
17 cm. medium *Minenwerfer*	Medium incendiary shell	1,126
	Medium gas shell	1,301
18 cm. smooth-bore *Minenwerfer*	Phosgene bomb	650 (?)

Nature.—Time and percussion.

Graduations.—Graduated from 7 to 21 in seconds and fifths of a second (lowest and highest figures are 7 and 21).

When the setting mark is opposite the cross, the fuze is set for percussion.

Material.—Brass body, with steel cap.

Remarks.—The original pattern of this fuze was marked Z.m.W.M., was identical in appearance and graduation, and only differed in its designation. The present pattern was introduced with a view to replacing Z.s.W.M. (*see* page 185) and providing a fuze which can be used with either the medium or the heavy *Minenwerfer*.

This fuze is so constructed that the percussion arrangement works equally well whether the projectile strikes the ground point first or base first. Should the percussion arrangement fail to act, detonation is effected by the time arrangement in the fuze, which for this purpose is set to act one or more seconds after impact.

The fuze cover used for night firing is shown in the plate. It is made of thin sheet iron, japanned black, and is screwed on to a flanged washer of the same metal, interposed between the fuze and the head of the shell.

---

* Approximate only.

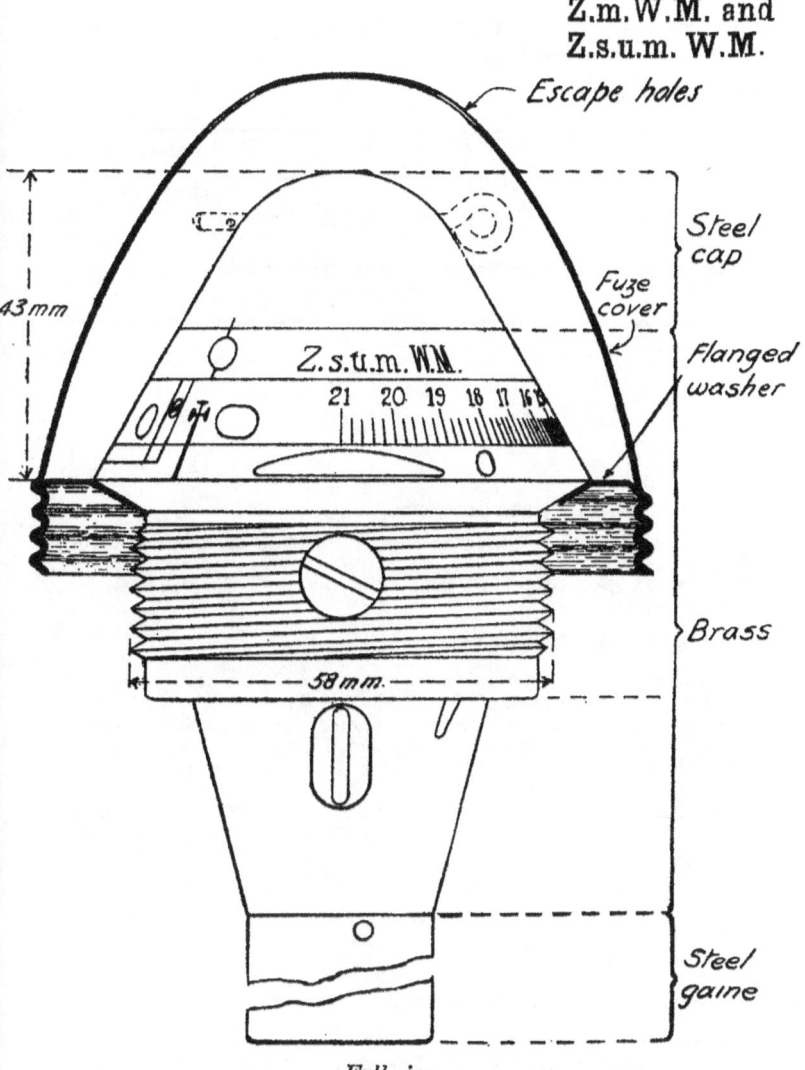

Designation.—*Z.s. W.M.* = *Zünder schwerer Wurf-Mine* (fuze for heavy *Minenwerfer* shell).

Used with.—

Minenwerfer.	Pattern of Shell.	Maximum range, time and percussion.
25 cm. heavy *Minenwerfer*	Full-sized heavy H.E. shell	yards. 514

Nature.—Time and percussion.

Graduations.—Graduated from 1* to 15 in seconds and fifths of a second.

When the setting mark is opposite the cross, the fuze is set for percussion.

Material.—Brass and aluminium.

Remarks.—This fuze is so constructed that the percussion arrangement works equally well whether the projectile strikes the ground point first or base first. Should the percussion arrangement fail to act, detonation is effected by the time arrangement in the fuze, which for this purpose is set to act one or more seconds after impact.

This fuze has been replaced by **Z.s.u.m.W.M.**, which is used with either the medium or the heavy *Minenwerfer*. *See* "Remarks" on page 182.

---

* In the latest patterns of this fuze, the graduations from 1 to 6 inclusive are omitted.

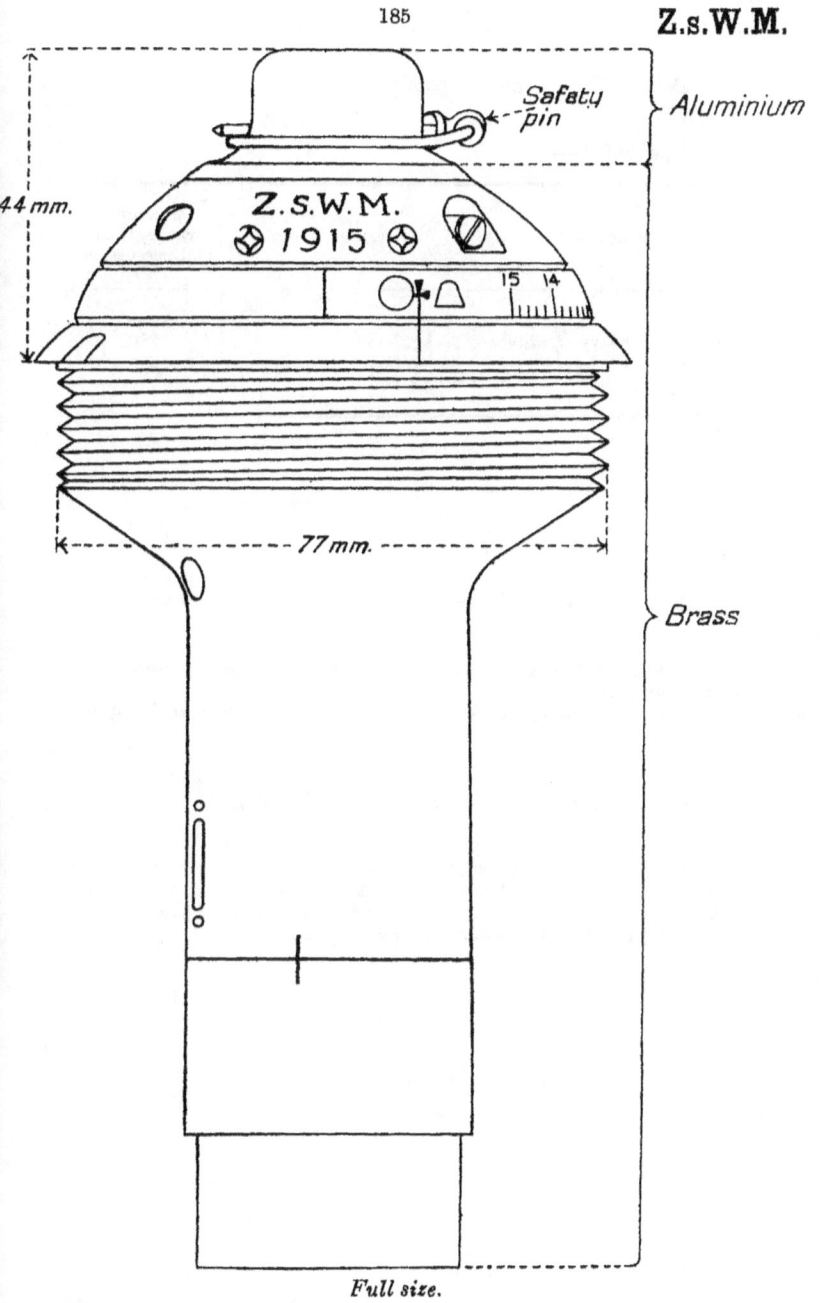

Full size.

Designation.—Canister bomb fuze.

Used with.—

Minenwerfer.	Pattern of Bomb.			Maximum range, time and percussion.
(25 cm.) heavy *Ladungs-werfer*, Ehrhardt	20 kg. bomb 30 kg. bomb 40 kg. bomb	... ...	... ...	yards. 280 208 175

Nature.—Time and percussion.

Graduations.—Graduated from 4 to 15 in seconds and fifths of a second.

When the setting mark is opposite the cross, the fuze is set for percussion.

Material.—Zinc with 2 brass rings and steel gaine.

Remarks.—The canister bomb with which this fuze is used is usually known as the "rum jar." It is made of thin sheet iron. A wooden slab is screwed on to the base to withstand the shock of discharge, and to act as a rough gas check.

Canister Bomb Fuze.

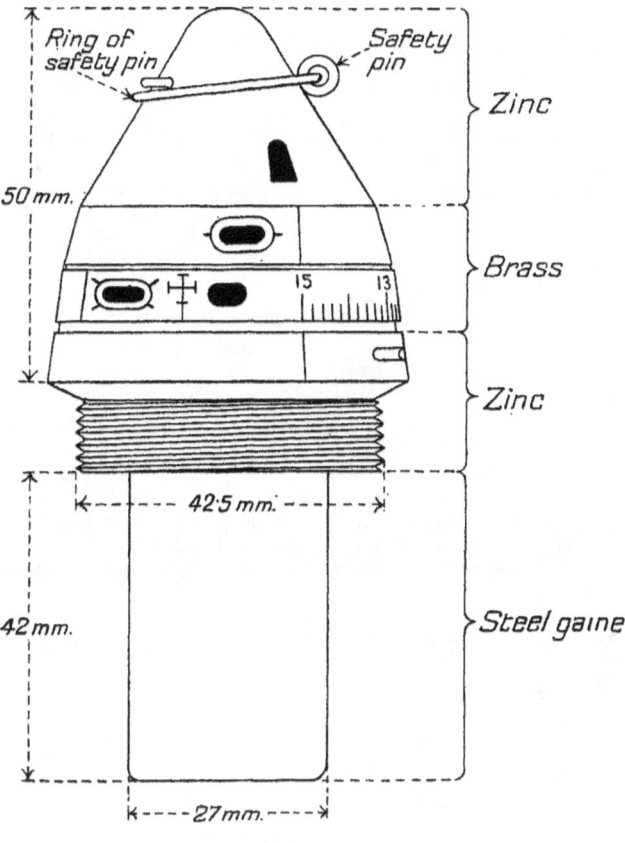

Full size.

Designation.—*Z.gl. W.M.* = *Zünder glatter Wurf-Mine* (fuze for smooth-bore *Minenwerfer* bomb).

Used with.—

Minenwerfer.	Pattern of Bomb.	Maximum range.	
		Time.	Perc'n.
18 cm. smooth-bore *Minenwerfer*	H.E. bomb	yards. 650 ?	yards. 650 ?

Nature.—Time and percussion.

Graduations.—Graduated from 7 to 21 in seconds and fifths of a second (lowest and highest figures are 7 and 21).
When the setting mark is opposite the cross, the fuze is set for percussion.

Material.—Body and cap of zinc alloy ; time rings of brass.

Remarks.—

Z.gl.W.M.

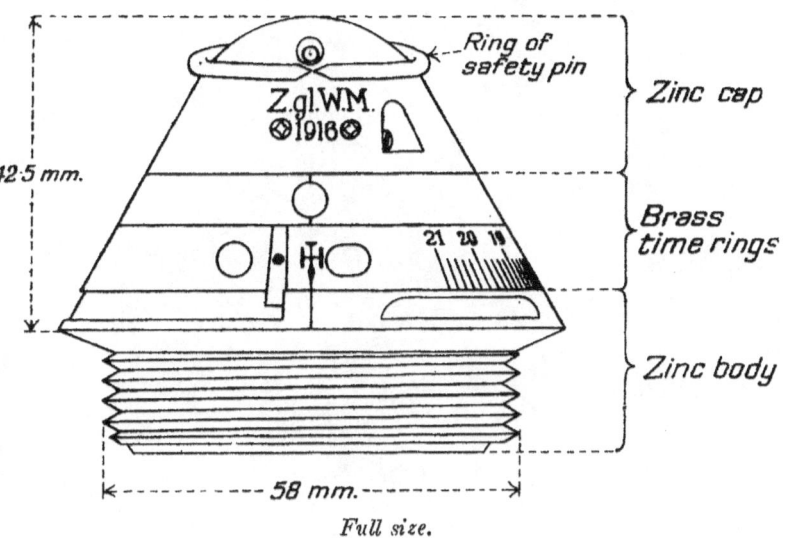

Full size.

194

FRENCH FUZES.

Designation.—

Fig. 1 *Fusée de 24/31, Modèle 1899.*
Fig. 2 *Fusée de 24/31, Modèle 1899–1908.*
Fig. 3 *Fusée I de 24/31, Modèle 1914.**

Used with.—

All three fuzes are used with :—

155 mm. gun	with "*Gaines-relais, Modèle*
120 mm. gun	*1915.*"
120 mm. gun	
95 mm. field gun, 1888	with "*Gaine-relais, Modèle*
90 mm. field gun, 1877	*1897–1914.*"
80 mm. field gun, 1877	

75 mm. field gun (with "*Détonateur, Modèle 1888*").

Nature.—Percussion.

Graduations.—Nil.

Material.—Brass.

Remarks.—The designation "Fusée de 24/31" is derived from the dimensions, *vide* Fig. 3.

The following manufacturers' marks may be found on these and similar fuzes.

ECP = Ecole Centrale de Pyrotechnie.
ATS = Atelier de Tarbes.
SFM = Société Française des Munitions de Chasse, de Tir et de Guerre.
SC = Naval Factory at St. Chamond.

⚓ T = Pyrotechnie Maritime de Toulon.

OTO = Société de l'Auto-Moto.

The figures "1–00" in Fig. 1 indicate the 1st batch manufactured in 1900.

---

* A similar fuze, viz., "*Fusée détonateur percutante de 22/31, Modèle 1915 (instantanée),*" is used with the 80, 90, and 120 mm. guns.

French Fuzes.—Percussion.

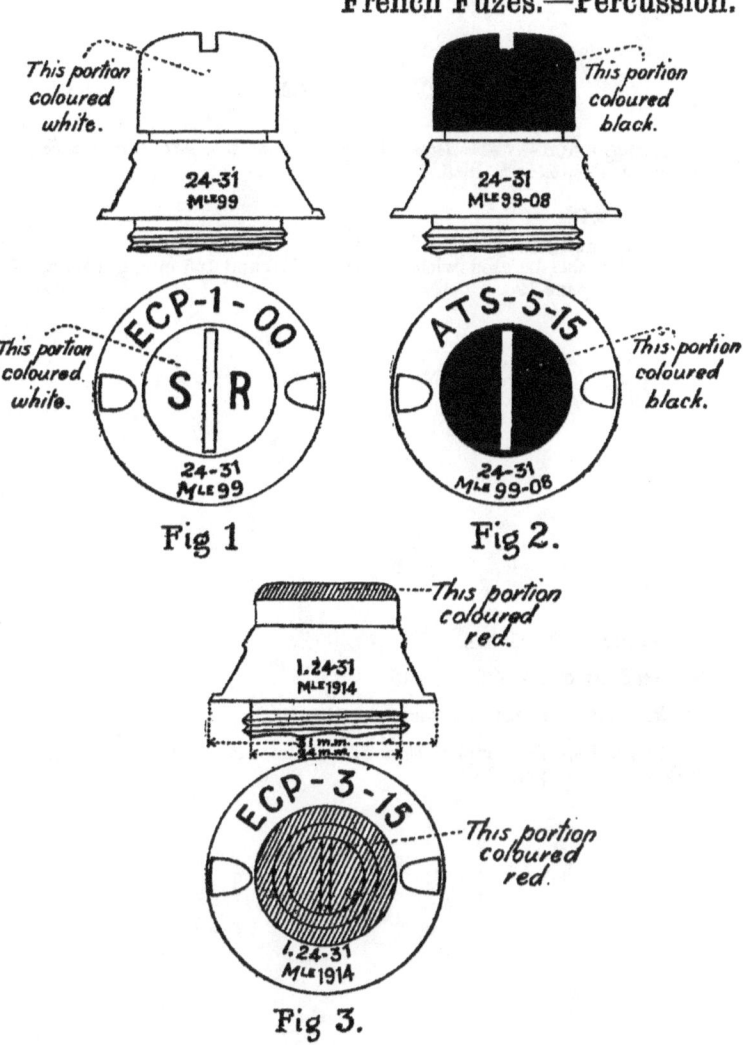

Fig 1.

Fig 2.

Fig 3.
Approx. full size.

FRENCH FUZE.

Designation.—*Fusée-détonateur percutante de 24/31, Instantanée allongée (IA), Modèle 1915.*

Used with.—
    75 mm. field gun : H.E. shell.
    Can also be used with 80, 90, 95, 120 and 155 mm. guns, *see* page 196.

Nature.—Percussion.

Graduations.—Nil.

Material.—Brass and steel.

Remarks.—For explanation of the marks on this fuze, *see* "Remarks" on page 196.

French Fuze. Percussion.

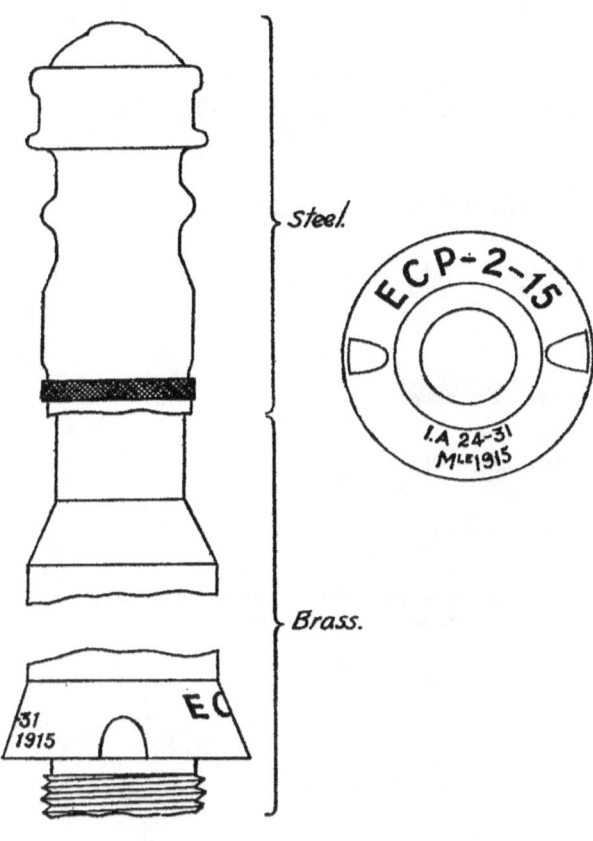

Full size.

FRENCH FUZE.

Designation.—*Fusée percutante de 30 S.M., Modèle 1878-81.*

Used with.—
Mortars of 220 mm. calibre and above.

Nature.—Percussion.

Graduations.—Nil.

Material.—Brass.

Remarks.—For explanation of the marks on this fuze, *see* "Remarks" on page 196.

French Fuze.
Percussion.

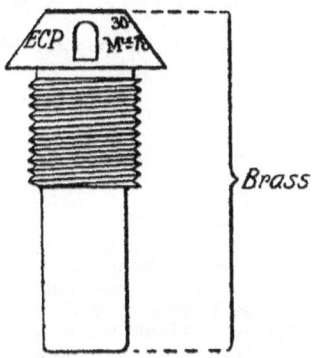

Brass

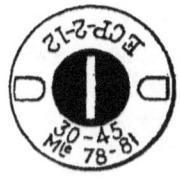

Scale ½

FRENCH FUZES.

Designation.—Fig. 1.   *Fusée à double effet de 22/31, Modèle 1897.**

Fig. 2.   *Fusée à double effet de 30/55, Modèle 1889.†*

Used with.—

Fig. 1 used with 75 mm. field gun : 1897, 1897A and 1897M patterns shrapnel.

Fig. 2 used with 155 mm., 120 mm. and 75 mm. guns.

Nature.—Time and percussion.

Graduations.—The fuzes are graduated in seconds and half-seconds by means of the oval holes on the spiral, as shown in the plate. Intermediate tenths of a second are indicated by four vertical lines between the large and small holes.

The setting of the fuze is indicated by a square hole punched in the spiral, the position of the left edge of this square hole giving the fuze-setting in tenths of a second.

In Fig. 1 the large holes are numbered from 1–24, and in Fig. 2, from 1–49, these numbers being equivalent to seconds.

Material.—Brass.

Remarks.—For manufacturers' marks borne by these fuzes, *see* "Remarks" on page 196.

---

* A similar fuze, viz., "*Fusée à double effet de 30/38, Modèle 1884*," is employed with 80 mm., 90 mm., 95 mm. and 120 mm. guns.

† Similar fuzes, viz., "*Fusée à double effet de siège de 30/55, Modèle 1882 M. 93*" and "*Fusée à double effet de siège de 40/55, Modèle 1880 M. 93*," are used with 120 mm. and 155 mm. guns, and mortars of 220 mm. and larger calibres.

French Fuzes.
Time and Percussion.

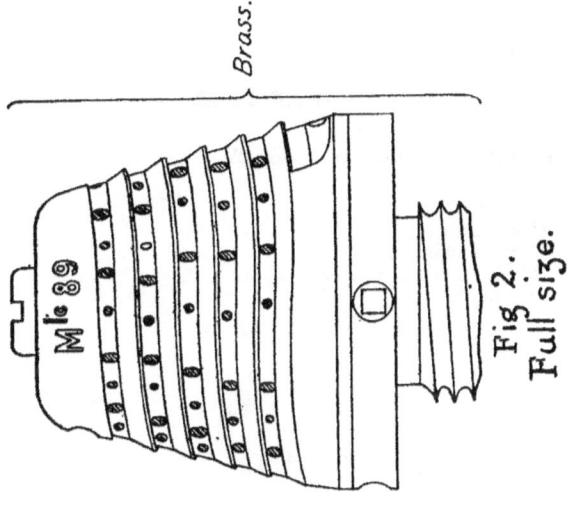

Fig. 2.
Full size.

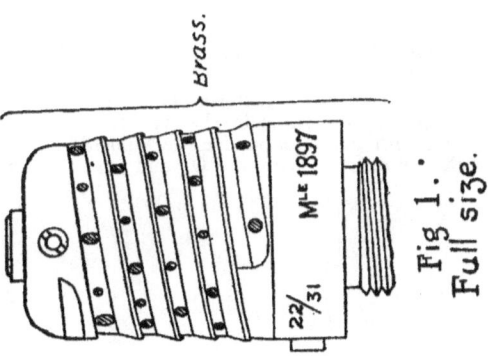

Fig. 1.
Full size.

BELGIAN FUZE.

Designation.—*Fusée à percussion de place.*

Used with.—
- 15 cm. gun.
- 15 cm. howitzer.
- 15 cm. mortar : range 4,265 yards.
- 12 cm. gun.

Nature.—Percussion.

Graduations.—Nil.

Material.—Brass.

Remarks.—The letters "EP" are typical of all Belgian fuzes (EP=*Ecole de Pyrotechnie*).

This fuze is made in three patterns, which are externally the same, but have slight differences in the strength of springs, etc. The pattern used with gun ammunition bears no additional mark, that used with howitzers is marked "O," and that with mortars "M."

Belgian Fuze.
Percussion.

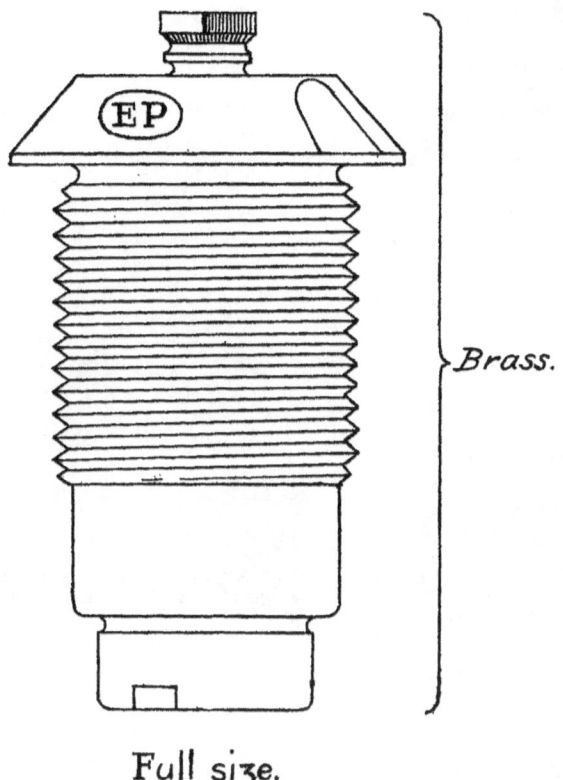

Brass.

Full size.

BELGIAN FUZE.

Designation.—*Fusée à percussion de campagne.*

Used with.—
    8·7 cm. gun.
    8·7 cm. howitzer.
    8·7 cm. mortar.
    7·5 cm. field gun (*à tir accéléré*).

Nature.—Percussion.

Graduations.—Nil.

Material.—Brass.

Remarks.—The letters "EP" are typical of all Belgian fuzes (EP=*Ecole de Pyrotechnie*). The figures "93" indicate **1893, the** year of manufacture.

Belgian Fuze.
Percussion.

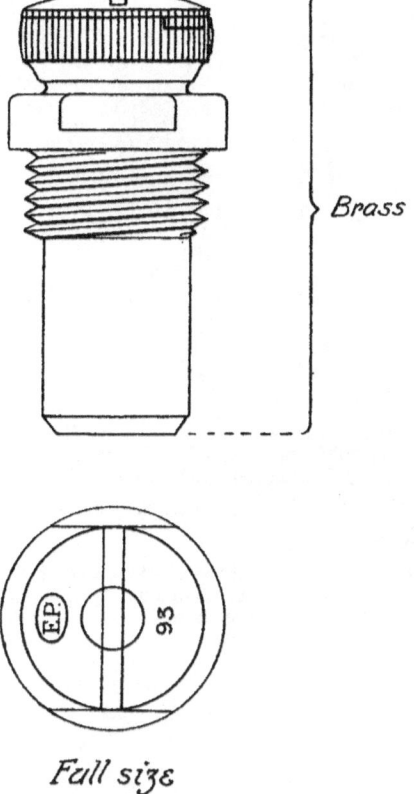

Brass

Full size

BELGIAN FUZE.

Designation.—*Fusée à temps de place.*

Used with.—

15 cm. gun (steel).
15 cm. howitzer.
15 cm. mortar.
12 cm. gun.

Nature.—Time.

Graduations.—Graduated from 1 to 20 (lowest and highest figures are 2 and 20) in half-seconds. When set to the 20 on the lowest ring, an additional 20 half-seconds is added to the time indicated by the upper scale.

Material.—Brass.

Remarks.—The milling on the head, and the fact of the figures being upside down, are typical of Belgian time fuzes. The letters "E P" are typical of all Belgian fuzes (E P = *Ecole de Pyrotechnie*).

Belgian Fuze.
Time.

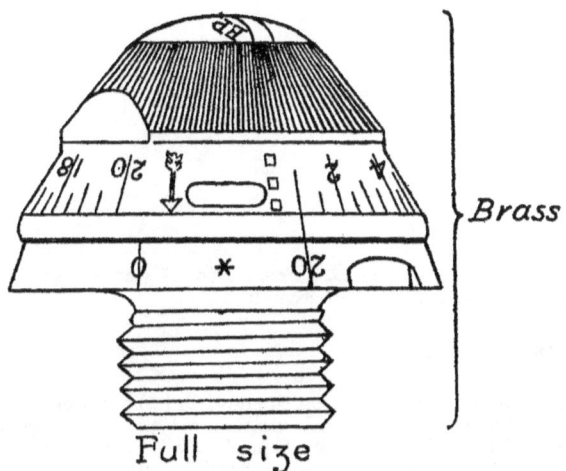

Brass

Full size

BELGIAN FUZE.

Designation.—*Fusée à temps de campagne.*

Used with.—
    8·7 cm. gun.
    8·7 cm. howitzer.
    8·7 cm. mortar.
    7·5 cm. field gun (*à tir accéléré*).

Nature.—Time.

Graduations.—Graduated from 1 to 28 (lowest and highest figures are 2 and 28) in half-seconds.

Material.—Brass.

Remarks.—The milling on the head and the fact of the figures of the time scale being upside down are typical of Belgian time fuzes. The letters "EP" are typical of all Belgian fuzes (EP = *Ecole de Pyrotechnie*). The figures "90" indicate 1890, the year of manufacture.

Belgian Fuze.
Time.

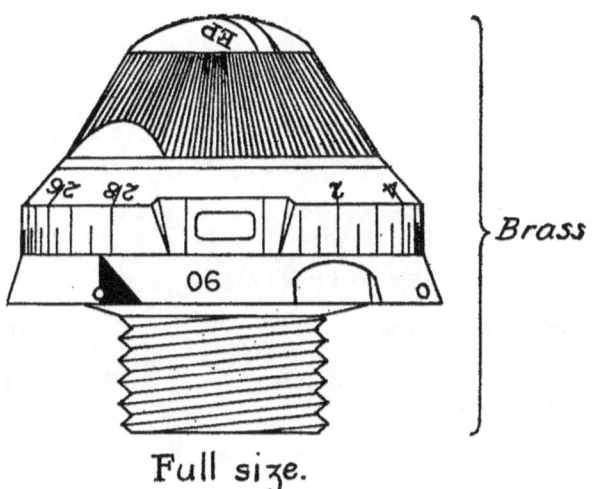

Brass

Full size.

BELGIAN FUZE.

Designation.—*Fusée à double effet de campagne.*

Used with.—
7·5 cm. field gun (*à tir rapide*).

Nature.—Time and percussion.

Graduations.—Graduated from 2 to 55 (lowest and highest figures are 2 and 54) in hundreds of metres (54=5,400 metres); each of the smallest divisions is equivalent to 50 metres of range.
Maximum (range time fuze) = 6,015 yards.

Material.—Aluminium.

Remarks.—The letters "EP" are typical of all Belgian fuzes (EP = *Ecole de Pyrotechnie*).

Belgian Fuze.
Time and Percussion.

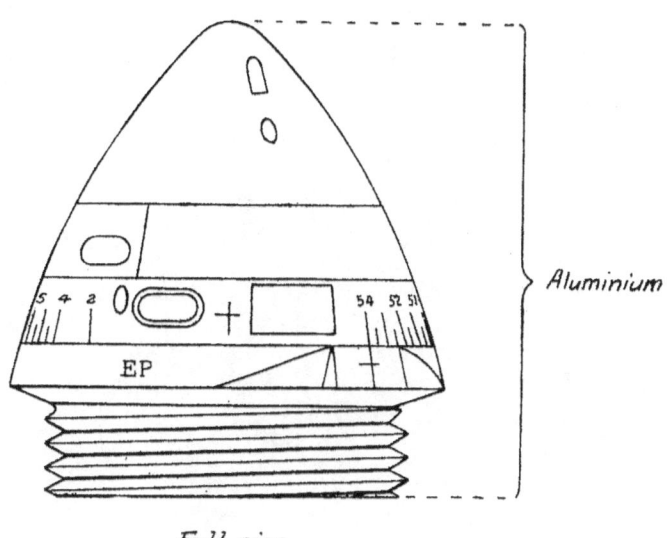

Full size

215

CONVERSION TABLE.

Inches to Millimetres.

1 inch = 25·3995411 millimetres.
1 millimetre = 0·03937708 inches.

Inches.	0	1/16	1/8	3/16	1/4	5/16	3/8	7/16	1/2	9/16	5/8	11/16	3/4	13/16	7/8	15/16	Inches.
0	0·000	1·587	3·175	4·762	6·350	7·937	9·525	11·112	12·700	14·287	15·875	17·462	19·050	20·637	22·225	23·812	0
1	25·400	26·987	28·574	30·162	31·749	33·337	34·924	36·512	38·099	39·687	41·274	42·862	44·449	46·037	47·624	49·212	1
2	50·800	52·387	53·974	55·561	57·149	58·736	60·324	61·911	63·499	65·086	66·674	68·261	69·849	71·436	73·024	74·611	2
3	76·199	77·786	79·374	80·961	82·549	84·136	85·723	87·311	88·898	90·486	92·073	93·661	95·248	96·836	98·423	100·011	3
4	101·59	103·19	104·77	106·35	107·95	109·53	111·13	112·71	114·30	115·89	117·47	119·06	120·65	122·24	123·83	125·41	4
5	127·00	128·58	130·17	131·75	133·35	134·94	136·53	138·11	139·70	141·28	143·67	144·85	146·05	147·63	149·22	150·81	5
6	152·40	153·98	155·57	157·15	158·75	160·34	161·93	163·51	165·10	166·68	168·27	169·85	171·45	173·03	174·62	176·21	6
7	177·80	179·38	180·97	182·55	184·15	185·73	187·33	188·91	190·50	192·08	193·67	195·25	196·85	198·43	200·02	201·61	7
8	203·20	204·78	206·37	207·95	209·55	211·13	212·73	214·31	215·90	217·48	219·07	220·65	222·25	223·83	225·42	227·01	8
9	228·60	230·18	231·77	233·35	234·95	236·53	238·13	239·71	241·30	243·00	244·07	246·05	247·65	249·23	250·82	252·41	9
10	254·00	255·58	257·17	258·76	260·35	261·93	263·52	265·11	266·70	268·28	269·87	271·46	273·05	274·63	276·22	277·81	10
11	279·40	280·98	282·57	284·16	285·75	287·33	288·92	290·51	292·10	293·68	295·27	296·85	298·44	300·03	301·62	303·21	11
12	304·80	306·38	307·97	309·56	311·14	313·73	314·32	315·91	317·50	319·08	320·67	322·25	323·84	325·43	327·02	328·61	12
13	330·20	331·78	333·37	334·97	336·55	338·13	339·72	341·31	342·90	344·48	346·07	347·66	349·25	350·83	352·42	354·01	13
14	355·60	357·18	358·77	360·36	361·94	363·53	365·12	366·71	368·30	369·88	371·47	373·06	374·64	376·23	377·82	379·41	14
15	380·99	382·58	384·17	385·76	387·34	388·93	390·52	392·10	393·69	395·28	396·87	398·45	400·04	401·63	403·22	404·81	15
16	406·40	407·98	409·58	411·16	412·75	414·33	415·92	417·51	419·10	420·68	422·27	423·85	425·45	427·03	428·62	430·20	16
17	431·79	433·38	434·97	436·55	438·14	439·73	441·32	442·90	444·49	446·08	447·67	449·25	450·84	452·43	454·02	455·60	17
18	457·19	458·78	460·37	461·96	463·54	465·13	466·72	468·30	469·89	471·48	473·07	474·65	476·24	477·83	479·42	481·00	18
19	482·59	484·18	485·77	487·35	488·94	490·53	492·12	493·70	495·29	496·88	498·47	500·05	501·58	503·23	504·82	506·40	19
20	507·99	509·58	511·17	512·75	514·34	515·93	517·52	519·10	520·69	522·28	523·87	525·45	527·04	528·63	530·22	531·80	20
21	533·39	534·98	536·57	538·15	539·74	541·33	542·92	544·50	546·09	547·68	549·27	550·85	552·44	554·03	555·61	557·20	21
22	558·79	560·38	561·97	563·55	565·14	566·73	568·32	569·90	571·49	573·08	574·67	576·25	577·84	579·43	581·01	582·60	22
23	584·19	585·78	587·37	588·95	590·54	592·13	593·72	595·30	596·89	598·48	600·07	601·65	603·24	604·83	606·41	608·00	23
24	609·59	611·18	612·77	614·35	615·94	617·53	619·11	620·70	622·29	623·88	625·46	627·05	628·64	630·23	631·81	633·40	24
25	634·99	636·58	638·16	639·75	641·34	643·93	644·51	646·10	647·69	649·28	650·86	652·45	654·04	655·63	657·21	658·80	25
26	660·39	661·98	663·57	665·15	666·74	668·33	669·91	671·50	673·09	674·68	676·27	677·85	679·44	681·03	682·61	684·20	26
27	685·79	687·38	688·97	690·55	692·14	693·73	695·31	696·90	698·49	700·08	701·66	703·25	704·84	706·43	708·01	709·60	27
28	711·19	712·78	714·36	715·95	717·54	719·13	720·71	722·30	723·89	725·47	727·06	728·65	730·24	731·83	733·41	735·00	28
29	736·59	738·17	739·76	741·35	742·94	744·53	746·11	747·70	749·29	750·87	752·46	754·05	755·64	757·22	758·81	760·40	29
30	761·99	763·57	765·16	766·75	768·34	769·93	771·51	773·10	774·69	776·27	777·86	779·45	781·04	782·63	784·21	785·80	30
31	787·39	788·97	790·56	792·15	793·74	795·33	796·91	798·50	800·09	801·67	803·26	804·85	806·44	808·03	809·61	811·20	31
32	812·79	814·37	815·96	817·55	819·14	820·73	822·31	823·90	825·49	827·07	828·66	830·25	831·84	833·43	835·01	836·60	32
33	838·19	839·77	841·36	842·95	844·54	846·13	847·71	849·30	850·89	852·47	854·06	855·65	857·24	858·83	860·41	862·00	33
34	863·59	864·97	866·55	868·14	869·73	871·52	873·11	874·70	876·28	877·57	879·46	881·05	882·63	884·22	885·80	887·40	34
35	888·98	890·57	892·16	893·75	894·93	896·52	898·11	900·70	901·28	903·27	904·86	906·45	908·03	909·62	911·21	913·80	35
36	914·38	915·97	917·56	919·15	920·73	922·32	923·91	925·50	927·08	928·67	929·26	931·85	933·43	935·02	936·61	938·20	36
37	939·78	941·37	942·96	944·55	946·13	947·72	949·31	950·90	952·48	954·07	955·66	957·25	958·83	960·42	962·01	963·60	37
38	965·18	966·77	968·36	969·95	971·53	973·12	974·71	976·30	977·88	979·47	981·06	982·65	984·23	985·82	987·41	988·99	38
39	990·58	992·17	993·76	995·34	996·93	998·52	1000·1	1001·7	1003·3	1004·9	1006·5	1008·0	1009·6	1011·2	1012·8	1014·4	39
40	1016·0	1017·6	1019·2	1020·7	1022·3	1023·9	1025·5	1027·1	1028·7	1030·3	1031·9	1033·4	1035·0	1036·6	1038·2	1039·8	40
41	1041·4	1043·0	1044·6	1046·1	1047·7	1049·3	1050·9	1052·5	1054·1	1055·7	1057·2	1058·8	1060·4	1062·0	1063·6	1065·2	41
42	1066·8	1068·4	1070·0	1071·5	1073·1	1074·7	1076·3	1077·9	1079·5	1081·1	1082·7	1084·2	1085·8	1087·4	1089·0	1090·6	42
43	1092·2	1093·8	1095·4	1096·9	1098·5	1100·1	1101·7	1103·3	1104·9	1106·5	1108·1	1109·6	1111·2	1112·8	1114·4	1116·0	43
44	1117·6	1119·2	1120·8	1122·3	1123·9	1125·5	1127·1	1128·7	1130·3	1131·9	1133·5	1135·0	1136·6	1138·2	1139·8	1141·4	44
45	1143·0	1144·6	1146·2	1147·7	1149·3	1150·9	1152·5	1154·1	1155·7	1157·3	1158·8	1160·4	1162·0	1163·6	1165·2	1166·8	45
46	1168·4	1170·0	1171·6	1173·1	1174·7	1176·3	1177·9	1179·5	1181·1	1182·7	1184·3	1185·9	1187·4	1189·0	1190·6	1192·2	46
47	1193·8	1195·4	1197·0	1198·5	1200·1	1201·7	1203·3	1204·9	1206·5	1208·1	1209·7	1211·2	1212·8	1214·4	1216·0	1217·6	47
48	1219·2	1220·8	1222·4	1223·9	1225·5	1227·1	1228·7	1230·3	1231·9	1233·5	1235·1	1236·6	1238·2	1239·8	1241·4	1243·0	48
49	1244·6	1246·2	1247·8	1249·3	1250·9	1252·5	1254·1	1255·7	1257·3	1258·9	1260·5	1262·0	1263·6	1265·2	1266·8	1268·4	49
Inches.	0	1/16	1/8	3/16	1/4	5/16	3/8	7/16	1/2	9/16	5/8	11/16	3/4	13/16	7/8	15/16	Inches.

APPENDIX II.

CONVERSION TABLE.

Yards to Metres.

Yards.	0	100	200	300	400	500	600	700	800	900
0	0	91	183	274	366	457	549	640	731	823
1,000	914	1,006	1,097	1,189	1,280	1,372	1,463	1,554	1,646	1,737
2,000	1,829	1,920	2,012	2,103	2,194	2,286	2,377	2,469	2,560	2,652
3,000	2,743	2,835	2,926	3,017	3,109	3,200	3,292	3,383	3,475	3,566
4,000	3,657	3,749	3,840	3,932	4,023	4,115	4,206	4,298	4,389	4,480
5,000	4,572	4,663	4,755	4,846	4,938	5,029	5,120	5,212	5,303	5,395
6,000	5,486	5,578	5,669	5,761	5,852	5,943	6,035	6,126	6,218	6,309
7,000	6,401	6,492	6,584	6,675	6,766	6,858	6,949	7,041	7,132	7,224
8,000	7,315	7,406	7,498	7,589	7,681	7,772	7,864	7,955	8,047	8,138
9,000	8,229	8,321	8,412	8,504	8,595	8,687	8,778	8,869	8,961	9,052
10,000	9,144	9,235	9,327	9,418	9,509	9,601	9,692	9,784	9,875	9,967
11,000	10,058	10,150	10,241	10,332	10,424	10,515	10,607	10,698	10,790	10,881
12,000	10,973	11,064	11,155	11,247	11,338	11,430	11,521	11,613	11,704	11,796
13,000	11,887	11,978	12,070	12,161	12,253	12,344	12,436	12,527	12,618	12,710
14,000	12,801	12,893	12,984	13,076	13,167	13,259	13,350	13,441	13,533	13,624
15,000	13,716	13,807	13,899	13,990	14,081	14,173	14,264	14,356	14,447	14,539
16,000	14,630	14,721	14,813	14,904	14,996	15,087	15,179	15,270	15,362	15,453
17,000	15,544	15,636	15,727	15,819	15,910	16,002	16,093	16,185	16,276	16,367
18,000	16,459	16,550	16,642	16,733	16,825	16,916	17,007	17,099	17,190	17,282
19,000	17,373	17,465	17,556	17,648	17,739	17,830	17,922	18,013	18,105	18,196
20,000	18,288	18,379	18,470	18,562	18,653	18,745	18,836	18,928	19,019	19,111
21,000	19,202	19,293	19,385	19,476	19,568	19,659	19,751	19,842	19,934	20,025

APPENDIX III.

CONVERSION TABLE.

Metres to Yards.

Metres.	0	100	200	300	400	500	600	700	800	900
0	0	109	219	328	437	547	656	765	875	984
1,000	1,094	1,203	1,312	1,422	1,531	1,640	1,750	1,859	1,968	2,078
2,000	2,187	2,297	2,406	2,515	2,625	2,734	2,843	2,953	3,062	3,171
3,000	3,280	3,390	3,500	3,609	3,718	3,828	3,937	4,046	4,156	4,265
4,000	4,374	4,484	4,593	4,703	4,812	4,921	5,031	5,140	5,249	5,359
5,000	5,468	5,577	5,687	5,796	5,906	6,015	6,124	6,234	6,343	6,452
6,000	6,562	6,671	6,780	6,890	6,999	7,109	7,218	7,327	7,437	7,546
7,000	7,655	7,765	7,874	7,983	8,093	8,202	8,312	8,421	8,530	8,640
8,000	8,749	8,858	8,968	9,077	9,186	9,296	9,405	9,515	9,624	9,733
9,000	9,843	9,952	10,061	10,171	10,280	10,389	10,499	10,608	10,718	10,827
10,000	10,936	11,046	11,155	11,264	11,374	11,483	11,592	11,702	11,811	11,920
11,000	12,030	12,139	12,249	12,358	12,467	12,577	12,686	12,795	12,905	13,014
12,000	13,124	13,233	13,342	13,452	13,561	13,670	13,780	13,889	13,998	14,108
13,000	14,217	14,327	14,436	14,545	14,655	14,764	14,873	14,983	15,092	15,201
14,000	15,311	15,420	15,530	15,639	15,748	15,858	15,967	16,076	16,186	16,295
15,000	16,404	16,514	16,623	16,732	16,842	16,951	17,061	17,170	17,279	17,389
16,000	17,498	17,607	17,717	17,826	17,936	18,045	18,154	18,264	18,373	18,482
17,000	18,592	18,701	18,810	18,920	19,029	19,139	19,248	19,357	19,467	19,576
18,000	19,685	19,795	19,904	20,013	20,123	20,232	20,342	20,451	20,560	20,670
19,000	20,779	20,888	20,998	21,107	21,216	21,326	21,435	21,545	21,654	21,763

www.ingramcontent.com/pod-product-compliance
Lightning Source LLC
Chambersburg PA
CBHW031253230426
43670CB00005B/163